CHRISTIANS
=== and the ===
MILITARY

For Ann,
with gratitude and
affection!

Bob Daly, S.J.

CHRISTIANS
and the
MILITARY

THE EARLY EXPERIENCE

John Helgeland
Robert J. Daly and
J. Patout Burns

edited by
Robert J. Daly

FORTRESS PRESS   PHILADELPHIA

Library of Congress Cataloging in Publication Data

Helgeland, John.
    Christians and the military.

    Bibliography: p.
    Includes index.
    1. War—Religious aspects—Christianity—History.
2. Church history—Primitive and early church, ca. 30-600.
I. Daly, Robert J., 1933-   . II. Burns, J. Patout.
III. Title.
BR195.W3H44   1985   261.8'73'09015   84-48718
ISBN 0-8006-1836-X

1267J84   Printed in the United States of America   1–1836

Contents

Acknowledgments

Material from Cicero, *De Officiis*, trans. Walter Miller, reprinted by permission of the publishers and The Loeb Classical Library, Cambridge, Mass.: Harvard University Press, 1913.

Material from Josephus, *The Jewish War*, trans. H. St. J. Thackeray, reprinted by permission of the publishers and The Loeb Classical Library, Cambridge, Mass.: Harvard University Press, 1927.

Material from *The Apostolic Fathers*, trans. Kirsopp Lake, reprinted by permission of the publishers and The Loeb Classical Library, Cambridge, Mass.: Harvard University, 1912.

Material from *Ante-Nicene Fathers*, reprinted by permission of William B. Eerdmanns Company.

Material from *The Treatise on the Apostolic Tradition of St. Hippolytus of Rome*, ed. G. Dix and H. Chadwick, © 1968 S.P.C.K. Reprinted by permission.

Material from *The Early Fathers on War and Military Service*, trans. Louis J. Swift, © 1983 Michael Glazier, Inc. Reprinted by permission.

Material from *New Testament Apocrypha, Volume One: Gospels and Related Writings*, by Edgar Hennecke; ed. Wilhelm Schneemelcher; English trans. ed. R. McL. Wilson. Copyright © 1959 J.C.B. Mohr (Paul Siebeck), Tübingen; English trans. © 1963 Lutterworth Press. Reprinted and used by the permission of The Westminster Press, Philadelphia, PA.

Material from *Roman Military Records on Papyrus*, trans. R.O. Fink, © 1971 American Philological Association. Reprinted by permission.

Foreword

This small book has its proximate origins in a two-day seminar at the June 1982 meeting of the Catholic Theological Society of America.[1] The strong positive reaction to that seminar prompted us to edit its material into the form of a long article. Fortress Press subsequently rescued us from the dilemma of having produced something too long for an article and too short for a book by inviting us to expand it, primarily by quoting the major texts cited, and to round it off into its present form. It is a genuinely coauthored work. No one of us could have produced it alone, and even those sections which have come primarily from the pen of one or the other of us have been refined in the crucible of our common discussion and criticism.[2] More remote, but hardly less important, our work is also due to the countless colleagues, students, and teachers whose interest and support have provided the foundation on which we built this small house. To all of them we acknowledge our debt.

The Authors

NOTES

1. Robert J. Daly, S.J., "Seminar on Patristics: Military Force and the Christian Conscience in the Early Church: A Methodological Approach," *Proceedings of the Thirty-seventh Annual Convention* (New York: Catholic Theological Society of America, 1982), 179–81.

2. Daly is primarily responsible for the introductory material, chaps. 2 and 6, and the general editing of the whole. Helgeland is primarily responsible for chaps. 1, 3–5, and 7–10. Burns is primarily responsible for chap. 11. The Conclusion was written by Burns and Daly.

Introduction

The intensification of the arms race and nuclear threat and the simultaneous growth of various peace movements, together with the association of some of these movements with traditional churches, most notably Roman Catholic, not previously associated with pacifism or conscientious objection, have all begun to increase the attention scholars are giving to the relationship of the Christian to the military. Biblical, patristic, and historical scholarship obviously owe this discussion not only the most accurate possible recording of the early church data on this topic, but also the most careful and critically contextualized interpretation of it. This, however, is a debt still unpaid. Most of those who have taken up the subject seem, consciously or unconsciously, to have done so more to support already-held positions than to find out what the situation in the early church really was.

A further complication has been a pacifist domination of English-speaking scholarship on the subject. This has generally resulted in a one-sided presentation of the evidence. Overly broad and uncritical pacifist assumptions often serve, ironically, to discredit pacifism and nonviolence and weaken the cause of peace. Among the more damaging of these is the assumption that the call to nonviolence has the identical meaning and extension as the call to avoid military service. This is simply not so. Early Christian attitudes toward military service seem to be at least ambiguous. But the evidence supporting the New Testament (NT) call to nonviolence, as we will see below, is overwhelming. Hence this assumption tends to create a massive anti-military-service bias in the way scholars interpret the early Christian data. Another damaging assumption is one that fails to distinguish between nonviolence and pacifism, or fails to recognize that pacifism, in its full sense, signifies a fully rounded religiophilosophical and political position—even though the word itself is often used to desig-

1

nate something far less than that. And finally there is the disastrous assumption which, rejecting or ignoring critical hermeneutics, assumes that NT and early Christian belief and practice are normative, at face value, for contemporary Christian life.

All these assumptions are sometimes summed up in the statement: "The early Christians were nonviolent and pacifist, therefore, we must be too." Unfortunately, history does not support such an absolutely stated premise; and even if it did, a sound theological hermeneutic would not allow one to draw such an unqualified conclusion. The conclusion may, for all that, still be true, but not *as* conclusion from *this* premise. Some of the purposes of this book are not only to bring more clarity to an important part of early Christian history, but also to serve the cause of peace by freeing the Christian ideal of pacifism and nonviolence from the weight of misread history and faulty reasoning that, in the long run, will only serve to discredit it.

1.

The Non-Christian Background
and the Political Situation
of the Life of the
Historical Jesus

Two witnesses from the non-Christian ancient world—the pagan, Cicero, and the Jew, Josephus—supply important parts of the background for our topic. Cicero's reflections are the starting point for all subsequent discussion in Western civilization on the question of a just war, and are the obvious source for much of Augustine's thought on the matter. Josephus's writings, written for the benefit of the Greek-reading public of the Roman Mediterranean world, provide us with an eyewitness view of the political and cultural situation in Palestine at the time when the NT was being formed.

Cicero
Marcus Tullius Cicero (106–43 B.C.E.), orator and statesman, gave some thought to the question of a just war, and what he said about it had widespread influence. Indeed, some of the lost portions of his work on this theme have been recovered in the work of St. Augustine (cf. *De republica* III, 35). As we see in the portion included below, there are two criteria for the declaration of the just war: self-defense and justice. The real context of Cicero's thinking about just war, however, was that of honor. On Cicero and, we may be sure, on many other Romans as well, the story of Regulus had made a deep impression. In the First Punic War, Regulus was freed from Carthage in order to negotiate the return of prisoners. Once safe in Rome, he refused to do this; but, since he had given his word as the condition of his release, he returned to face death in Carthage. Under the cry of "Carthago delenda est" ("Carthage must be destroyed") the Romans pressed on to victory.

Cicero emphasized that war must be fought with honor in every case except with pirates—a promise given to a pirate is not binding since pirates are not a legally constituted nation (*De officiis* III, 107). The conduct of the war was not to be unnecessarily cruel since cruelty

3

helps nothing. It was the fetial priesthood which Cicero recognized as the authority in the declaration and conduct of the just war (*De officiis* III, 108, and *De republica* II, 31). He cites, moreover, one case in which an unrighteous victory had blemished a righteous cause (*De officiis* II, 27).

Cicero does not go beyond setting down criteria, which are not elaborate, for the just war. For him as well as for Augustine who borrowed from him, the presupposition that wars will always be necessary was never in doubt. Nor is there any regret about the casualties or the destruction in these wars if they are in fact justly declared and conducted. Perhaps for Cicero this presupposition derives from his conception of natural law. For example, youth is a time to obey, to avoid sensuous pleasures, and to prepare for military and civil service—whereas the later years are reserved for less labor and more exercise of wisdom based upon experience (*De officiis* I, 122).

11. Again, there are certain duties that we owe even to those who have wronged us. For there is a limit to retribution and to punishment; or rather, I am inclined to think, it is sufficient that the aggressor should be brought to repent of his wrong-doing, in order that he may not repeat the offence and that others may be deterred from doing wrong.

Then, too, in the case of a state in its external relations, the rights of war must be strictly observed. For since there are two ways of settling a dispute: first, by discussion; second, by physical force; and since the former is characteristic of man, the latter of the brute, we must resort to force only in case we may not avail ourselves of discussion. The only excuse, therefore, for going to war is that we may live in peace unharmed; and when the victory is won, we should spare those who have not been blood-thirsty and barbarous in their warfare. For instance, our forefathers actually admitted to full rights of citizenship the Tusculans, Aequians, Volscians, Sabines, and Hernicians, but they razed Carthage and Numantia to the ground. I wish they had not destroyed Corinth; but I believe they had some special reason for what they did—its convenient situation, probably—and feared that its very location might some day furnish a temptation to renew the war. In my opinion, at least, we should always strive to secure a peace that shall not admit of guile. And if my advice had been heeded on this point, we should still have at least some sort of constitutional government, if not the best in the world, whereas, as it is, we have none at all.

Not only must we show consideration for those whom we have conquered by force of arms but we must also ensure protection to those who lay down their arms and throw themselves upon the mercy of our generals, even though the battering-ram has hammered at their walls. And among our countrymen justice has been observed so conscientiously in this direction, that those who have given promise of protection to states or nations subdued in war become, after the custom of our forefathers, the patrons of those states.

As for war, humane laws touching it are drawn up in the fetial code of the

Roman People under all the guarantees of religion; and from this it may be gathered that no war is just, unless it is entered upon after an official demand for satisfaction has been submitted or warning has been given and a formal declaration made. Popilius was general in command of a province. In his army Cato's son was serving on his first campaign. When Popilius decided to disband one of his legions, he discharged also young Cato who was serving in that same legion. But when the young man out of love for the service stayed on in the field, his father wrote to Popilius to say that if he let him stay in the army, he should swear him into service with a new oath of allegiance, for in view of the voidance of his former oath he could not legally fight the foe. So extremely scrupulous was the observance of the laws in regard to the conduct of war. There is extant, too, a letter of the elder Marcus Cato to his son Marcus, in which he writes that he has heard that the youth has been discharged by the consul, when he was serving in Macedonia in the war with Perseus. He warns him, therefore, to be careful not to go into battle; for, he says, the man who is not legally a soldier has no right to be fighting the foe.

12. This also I observe—that he who would properly have been called "a fighting enemy" (*perduellis*) was called "a guest" (*hostis*), thus relieving the ugliness of the fact by a softened expression; for "enemy" (*hostis*) meant to our ancestors what we now call "stranger" (*peregrinus*). This is proved by the usage in the Twelve tables: "Or a day fixed for trial with a stranger" (*hostis*). And again: "Right of ownership is inalienable for ever in dealings with a stranger" (*hostis*). What can exceed such charity, when he with whom one is at war is called by so gentle a name? And yet long lapse of time has given that word a harsher meaning: for it has lost its signification of "stranger" and has taken on the technical connotation of "an enemy under arms."

But when a war is fought out for supremacy and when glory is the object of war, it must still not fail to start from the same motives which I said a moment ago were the only righteous grounds for going to war. But those wars which have glory for their end must be carried on with less bitterness. For we contend, for example, with a fellow-citizen in one way, if he is a personal enemy, in another, if he is a rival: with the rival it is a struggle for office and position, with the enemy for life and honor. So with the Celtiberians and the Cimbrians we fought as with deadly enemies, not to determine which should be supreme, but which should survive; but with the Latins, Sabines, Samnites, Carthaginians, and Pyrrhus we fought for supremacy. The Carthaginians violated treaties; Hannibal was cruel; the others were more merciful. From Pyrrhus we have this famous speech on the exchange of prisoners:

"Gold will I none, nor price shall ye give; for I ask none;
Come, let us not be chaff'rers of war, but warriors embattled.
Nay; let us venture our lives, and the sword, not gold, weigh the
outcome.
Make we the trial by valor in arms and see if Dame Fortune
Wills it that ye shall prevail or I, or what be her judgment.
Hear thou, too, this word, good Fabricius: whose valor soever
Spared hath been by the fortune of war—their freedom I grant them.
Such my resolve. I give and present them to you, my brave Romans;
Take them back to their homes; the great gods' blessings attend you."
A rightly kingly sentiment this and worthy a scion of the Aeacidae.

13. Again, if under stress of circumstances individuals have made any promise to the enemy, they are bound to keep their word even then. For instance, in the First Punic War, when Regulus was taken prisoner by the Carthaginians, he was sent to Rome on parole to negotiate an exchange of prisoners; he came and, in the first place, it was he that made the motion in the senate that the prisoners should not be restored; and in the second place, when his relatives and friends would have kept him back, he chose to return to a death by torture rather than prove false to his promise, though given to an enemy.

And again in the Second Punic War, after the Battle of Cannae, Hannibal sent to Rome ten Roman captives bound by an oath to return to him, if they did not succeed in ransoming his prisoners; and as long as any one of them lived, the censors kept them all degraded and disfranchised, because they were guilty of perjury in not returning. And they punished in like manner the one who had incurred guilt by an evasion of his oath: with Hannibal's permission this man left the camp and returned a little later on the pretext that he had forgotten something or other; and then, when he left the camp the second time, he claimed that he was released from the obligation of his oath; and so he was, according to the letter of it, but not according to the spirit. In the matter of a promise one must always consider the meaning and not the mere words.

Our forefathers have given us another striking example of justice toward an enemy: when a deserter from Pyrrhus promised the senate to administer poison to the king and thus work his death, the senate and Gaius Fabricius delivered the deserter up to Pyrrhus. Thus they stamped with their disapproval the treacherous murder even of an enemy who was at once powerful, unprovoked, aggressive, and successful.

With this I will close my discussion of the duties connected with war. (*De officiis* I, 11–13)

Josephus

At times during the lifetime of Jesus, the province of Judea saw violent conflicts between the Jews and the Romans. The first of these took place in the year A.D. 6 when the procurator Coponius began to conduct a taxation. Judas the Galilean revolted and encouraged many of his countrymen to do the same. It is the common opinion that Judas was the founder of the party of the Zealots who eventually sparked the war with Rome in the years 66–70. But, since Josephus does not use the term "zealot" to designate a political party until the sixties, the connection between Judas and the Zealots of later is obscure.[1] Nevertheless, it is clear that Judas urged many to violent opposition to Rome on the grounds that paying tribute is owed only to God, thereby implicitly granting the Romans divine status. Old Testament (OT) custom held that God was the owner of the land and that tribute was to be given to him only.

The following passage is from Josephus, a Jewish general captured in the war of 66–70. Taken to Rome, he wrote extensively about the relationships between Jews and Romans. One of his apologetic concerns in his work was to show that the relationships between Jerusalem and Rome were upset at the hands of dissident groups and not by the Jewish people as a whole. Thus, he tends to highlight small bands of disaffected people such as Judas and his followers.

The territory of Archelaus was now reduced to a province, and Coponius, a Roman of the equestrian order, was sent out as procurator, entrusted by Augustus with full powers, including the infliction of capital punishment. Under his administration, a Galilean, named Judas, incited his countrymen to revolt, upbraiding them as cowards for consenting to pay tribute to the Romans and tolerating mortal masters, after having God for their lord. This man was a sophist who founded a sect of his own, having nothing in common with the others. (*Jewish War* II, 117–18)

In the year 26, Pontius Pilate, sent by the emperor Tiberius, arrived in Jerusalem. His entrance, characteristic of his administration in Judea, is the first of a series of upsetting incidents. By night he brought Roman army standards into the holy city. Behind the Jewish objection to these standards was their religious, and from the Jewish perspective, idolatrous character. In them resided the numinous power of the legion, and some of them contained a bust of the emperor.[2] The Jews employed passive resistance, refusing the perhaps hopeless tack of locking in combat with the Roman troops. Unwilling to provoke active resistance from the Jews, Pilate followed the policy of his predecessors and took the hated standards out of the city.

The next incident turned to blood. Pilate had confiscated the temple funds, *Corbonas* (see Matt. 27:6), and built an aqueduct with them. When this got out, the Jews angrily pressed in on his entourage. He prepared for them by disguising legionnaires as civilians and arming them with bludgeons. Whether by clubbing or being trampled, many of the demonstrators were killed in the riot.

Pilate, being sent by Tiberius as procurator to Judaea, introduced into Jerusalem by night and under cover the effigies of Caesar which are called standards. This proceeding, when day broke, aroused immense excitement among the Jews; those on the spot were in consternation, considering their laws to have been trampled under foot, as those laws permit no image to be erected in the city; while the indignation of the townspeople stirred the countryfolk, who flocked together in crowds. Hastening after Pilate to Caesarea, the Jews implored him to remove the standards from Jerusalem and to uphold the laws of their ancestors. When Pilate refused, they fell prostrate around his house and for five whole days and nights remained motionless in that position. On the ensuing day Pilate took his seat on his tribunal in the great stadium and summoning the multitude, with the apparent intention of answering them, gave the arranged signal to his armed soldiers to surround the Jews. Finding themselves in a ring of troops, three deep, the Jews were struck dumb at this unexpected sight. Pilate, after threatening to cut them down if they refused to admit Caesar's images, signalled to the soldiers to draw their swords. Thereupon the Jews, as by concerted action, flung themselves in a body on the ground, extended their necks, and exclaimed that they were ready rather to die than to transgress the law. Overcome with astonishment at such intense religious zeal, Pilate gave orders for the immediate removal of the standards from Jerusalem.

On a later occasion he provoked a fresh uproar by expending upon the construction of an aqueduct the sacred treasure known as *Corbonas;* the water was brought from a distance of 400 furlongs. Indignant at this proceeding the populace formed a ring round the tribunal of Pilate, then on a visit to Jerusalem, and besieged him with angry clamor. He, foreseeing the tumult, had interspersed among the crowd a troop of his soldiers, armed but disguised in civilian dress, with orders not to use their swords, but to beat any rioters with cudgels. He now from his tribunal gave the agreed signal. Large numbers of the Jews perished, some from the blows which they received, others trodden to death by their companions in the ensuing flight. Cowed by the fate of the victims, the multitude was reduced to silence. (*Jewish War* II, 169–77)

Josephus knew about the Christian movement. Still we find in his work no reference to Christians engaging in violence. If we keep in mind Josephus's apologetic stance toward Rome, it seems likely that he would have been all too ready to report any such activity on their part. From the Christian side, the gospels report little about the political violence in their time. There is only the obscure reference to "the Galileans whose blood Pilate had mingled with their sacrifices" (Luke 13:1). Josephus tells about some Samaritans whom Pilate slaughtered while they were going to Mt. Gerizim to see some sacred vessels supposedly buried there by Moses.[3] Probably these are not the same incident. That on Mt. Gerizim happened in the year 36, after Jesus' death.

There have been some attempts to connect Jesus with revolutionary movements. The best argument on this direction has been the work of S. G. F. Brandon whose book *Jesus and the Zealots,* however, has not withstood the wrath of the reviewers.[4] The references to the disciples carrying swords ("And they said, 'Look, Lord, here are two swords.' And he said to them, 'It is enough.' " Luke 22:38) do not prove that the disciples were revolutionaries. They could have carried swords, as did the Essenes, for personal protection while traveling on the highway. At any rate, two swords would scarcely have threatened the Romans. Overturning the tables of the money-changers in the temple, too, was not much of a revolutionary act even if the temple was protected by the Romans (Mark 11:15–17 par.). Such a display was more akin to the "body language" of the prophets of ancient Israel, a "prophetic parabolic action" as Hengel calls it.[5] The suggestion that Jesus was crucified as a revolutionary, though, is probably true enough: the superscription over the cross read "King of the Jews." This, however, does not prove that Jesus was a revolutionary, but only that the Romans thought so or at least were not taking any chances with someone attracting a following. The same caution can be seen in Pilate's slaughtering the demonstrators and the Samaritans on Mt. Gerizim. Since Jesus was crucified between two *lēstai* (the word can mean "brigand," "robber," or "insurrectionist") some have hastily concluded that the Romans had proof that Jesus was a revolutionary. Still, guilt by association proves nothing. The balance of the evidence points in other directions.

In view of the fact that the parables of the kingdom of God are among those portions of the gospel sayings of Jesus most likely to be authentic and that these sayings deal with a forgiving father and his willingness to love everyone, it would seem that Jesus never intended a political revolution. In fact, Jesus' view of the nature of the coming kingdom seems to be formulated to counter those of some of his more apocalyptic contemporaries. Consequently, the most violent statement which might legitimately be distilled from the gospels is that Jesus permitted his followers to carry swords in defense against highwaymen.

NOTES

1. Morton Smith, "Zealots and Sicarii, Their Origins and Relation," *Harvard Theological Review* 64 (1971): 1–19.

2. Carl H. Kraeling, "The Episode of the Roman Standards at Jerusalem," *Harvard Theological Review* 35 (1942): 263–89.

3. *Jewish Antiquities* 18.85–87.

4. New York: Charles Scribner's Sons, 1967. See also the reviews: Smith, "Zealots and Sicarii"; Martin Hengel, *Journal of Semitic Studies* 14 (1969): 231–40; Walter Wink, *Union Seminary Quarterly Review* 25 (1969): 37–57.

5. Hengel, 237.

2.

The New Testament Background

Modern biblical studies and, especially in recent years, the application of sociological analysis, have greatly broadened the way intelligent readers must now approach the NT. For example, with regard to texts that may have a bearing on issues such as nonviolence or military force, one cannot discover what a Christian should do today simply from a face-value, biblicist reading of the NT. Nevertheless, certain valid biblical-theological conclusions (at least in the form of general action principles or general directions of Christian commitment) can, with care, be drawn. There has also been some success in applying sociological analysis to NT texts and the situations of the NT communities. As one moves into the period of the early church, however, such success becomes vastly more difficult to achieve. The data to be analyzed are immeasurably greater, far more complex, and often not easily accessible. And patristic scholarship is only beginning to take up the massive task of applying critical methods of analysis to the changing sociological and political situations of the patristic age. This book is an attempt to analyze, in the light of the biblical background and in its own sociopolitical context, the early Christian experience of war and military service up to the time of Augustine.

The Love Command and Nonviolence

Arguing from biblical and early church data, sometimes from precisely the same data, various authors have claimed support for almost every conceivable position from radical pacifism to holy war. Obviously something is wrong with the scholarship involved—unless one is willing to accept that the NT is hopelessly contradictory and devoid of authority on this point. A further embarrassment for scholarship is that, in most cases, one need only know an author's confessional position in order to know the results of his or her analysis. So much for the ideals of objectivity and an unprejudiced, value-free reading of the data! Clearly, unless one is ready to retreat in despair, a much more rigorous method of analysis is called for. A summary of such a method can be reduced to various aspects of the following four questions:

1. What are the data, the facts, and how does one gain access to them?

2. How are these data to be interpreted in their various (historical, theological, political, sociological, etc.) contexts?

3. What is the significance of these data for us today?

4. How does one's bias and presuppositions, one's theology and confessional allegiance affect one's perception, interpretation, and determination of the significance of these data?

For the modern Christian who is attempting to formulate a position in the light of the Bible and early church, attention to all four of these questions and to the connections between them is essential. Modern writers, however, have tended to concentrate only on the third of these questions, badly neglecting the other three. They have falsely assumed that the task of questions one and two, research into and interpretation of the data, had already been adequately done. And they have generally compounded this weakness by not rigorously raising the fourth question about the influence of their own bias and presuppositions.

The solution, however, is not as easy as this brief analysis suggests. For Christians who give some thought to these issues generally think or feel that what they believe and try to live by as Christians must be validated by being found to be in straightforward harmony not just with the Bible but also with the teaching and practice of the fathers and the early church. The almost invariable result is that early Christian data are read and interpreted selectively and in the light of one's already-held position, instead of openly and with a view to criticizing and possibly correcting one's position.

The early fathers, as is obvious from the anguished discussions that preceded Nicaea's *homoousion* (the doctrine, not expressly taught in the Scripture, that the Son is *consubstantial* with the Father), saw themselves as faithfully adhering to the biblical witness. This was especially true regarding the teaching of Jesus recorded and reflected in the NT. Now the question of nonviolence, which is closely associated by implication with that of military service, is one of the relatively few living questions to which the teaching of Jesus recorded in the NT seems to give direct attention. Hence, critical knowledge of the biblical data is foundational for a fully adequate, critical interpretation of the patristic data. This does not mean that every patristic scholar must also be a biblical exegete; but it does mean that, unless sound critical knowledge of the Bible forms an integral part of the background that theology brings to the work of applying early Christian witness to contemporary Christian life, the theological task is not complete. It is a fact that patristic interpretations of Scripture sometimes differ from contemporary critical interpretations (just as aspects of ancient Christian practice sometimes differ from aspects of modern Christian practice). Analyzing and making sense of where and how and why this is so constitutes one of the most important tasks of the theologian.

On our theme, modern exegetes generally agree with the ancient fathers that, however differently one may try to apply it in practice, the basic thrust of the Lord's teaching is clearly toward nonviolence. Ironically, however, this scholarly agreement can sometimes lead to false conclusions. For from the apparent fact that Christ preached nonviolence as a basic attitude for his followers, many assume a negative answer to the question of Christians serving in the military. But this is not a strictly logical or theological conclusion, nor does history, when carefully examined, provide a strong case that early Christians generally thought so. The biblical evidence, especially when one includes the whole NT and its various contexts, is simply not univocal in its witness on this point. And when one examines the data apart from pacifist assumptions, one finds, as we will indicate below, that Christ's teaching on nonviolence was not interpreted or put into practice in a univocally pacifist or anti-military-service way by the fathers and the early Christians.

The ideal scholarly response to this situation would be to apply to the patristic data the same methodological thoroughness and sophistication that NT exegetes now commonly bring to their work: text criticism, source criticism, history of traditions, form criticism, redaction criticism, literary criticism, structural criticism, hermeneutics, sociological analysis, etc. Since exegetes themselves often do not control all these methods, however, one can hardly expect the patristic scholar to master them and then apply them to the immeasurably more vast body of patristic data. But if one were to suggest where we might best begin, it might well be with sociological analysis. Our theme has broad sociological ramifications, and the sociological analysis of early Christian data has recently begun to receive extensive critical attention. We need to spend a great deal more time seeking precise answers to questions like: What is being said, taught, handed on, reported, etc., and why? What kind of authority does the author attribute to what is being said, taught, handed on, reported, etc.? What are the theological, religious, historical, political, and sociological situations of the text (or event) being studied? of the situations in which the text arose? of the persons and communities who received and handed on the text? Is the text (or event) typical or characteristic of what may be described as a central Christian stance? for its own time? for later times? Or is it peripheral to the mainstream? for its own or later times?

A good place to begin such an analysis is with the love command and the call to nonviolence in the NT.[1] Identifying Matt. 5:38–48, Luke 6:27–36, and Rom. 12:14, 17, 19–21 as key texts leaves us well within an exegetical consensus. The text from Romans, "Bless those who persecute you; bless and do not curse. . . . Repay no one evil for evil. . . . Beloved, never avenge yourselves, but leave it to the wrath," was written in the late 50s. It contains variations that suggest an independent line of a tradition derived from Jesus and formulated in a Pauline manner, and it clearly contains the same teaching as Matthew and Luke, written some two or three decades later. Both Matt. 5:38–48 (from the Sermon on the Mount) and its parallel in Luke 6:27–36 (from the shorter Lukan sermon) come from the hypothetical Q document which, together with the Gospel of Mark, was one of the two main outside sources from which, in the opinion of most critical exegetes, Matthew and Luke respectively composed their gospels.[2] Increasing attention is now being given to this Q document, to the community attitudes that shaped it, and to the theology implied in it. But the tensions between the practical demands of life in the world and an eschatologically oriented interim ethic cannot be resolved on the basis of a hypothetical Q. For this a wider context than even just the NT texts is needed; one must look also to the understanding and practice of the early church.

But the beginning of this wider context is precisely Matt. 5:38–48 and Luke 6:27–36 which record Jesus' teaching on nonviolence. And it is indeed the gospels, not a hypothetical Q (which no one before the nineteenth century was even aware of) nor any necessarily hypothetical reconstruction of the original sayings of Jesus, that Christians from the age of the fathers to our own day revere as God's Word. What we can piece together of the Matthean and Lukan communities which produced these respective gospels indicates that there was a strong, but by now diminishing expectation of an imminent Parousia. These were communities that were beginning to settle down for the long haul. Ultimately, our inquiry comes down to two interrelated questions that might, of course, be just one question: What did Matt. 5:38–48 and Luke 6:27–36 mean in their respective gospel contexts? What do they mean for us today?

One is still on relatively sure ground in rejecting, as not doing justice to the text, those existential interpretations of the love command and call to nonviolence that center on what goes on internally in the heart of the one who loves. What does do justice to the text is the view that the Christian is really looking to the effect that nonviolence will have in the heart of the enemy. This sees love of the enemy as a concrete social event.[3] One should note, however, that this is not a universally applicable ethical rule, but the attitude expected of Christians when they encounter resistance. It can be practiced only by the weak toward the strong. Only those involved in the resistance of the weak toward the strong can preach or demand it. When it is recommended or imposed from outside, it is perverted into a demand to give up resistance (cf. Schottroff, 13).

This understanding of love for the enemy can be verified as a valid interpretation of Matt. 5:38–48 and Luke 6:27–36. But if love of enemy is not passive, but is rather an active seeking to convert the enemy, to turn evil into good, how can we explain it in relation to the clear prohibition of resistance in Matt. 5:38–41 and Luke 6:29? Why is resistance forbidden and active love of the enemy enjoined? To see this merely or primarily as an attack on the zealot position does not make much sense chronologically. But there are clear political implications in this. To see what they might be requires one to see the call both to renounce resistance to evil *and* actively to love the enemy in the context of the ways in which antiquity conceived "loving one's enemy."

In non-Christian antiquity, one can find at least three somewhat parallel situations and themes. There is the renunciation of revenge by the powerful. Whether motivated by magnanimity or political expediency, this reflects a situation fundamentally different from that of the earliest Christians. (But one should note that when Christians do come into power, their teachers, as we see in Ambrose and Augustine, also exhort to magnanimity.) Then there is the philosopher's (e.g., Socrates) nonviolent protest or acceptance of abuse in order to proclaim the rottenness of society. This is obviously not what is going on in the gospels. Finally there are the attitudes and reactions of the powerless underdog. This does fit the situation of the early Christians. Yet no early Christian source pays any attention to the social situation of dependence that gave Christians no other option but to submit to injustice peaceably. Thus the question, on this level, remains open: Is this a universal ethic for everyone, or only for Christians in a similar situation of powerlessness? This is obviously a key question for Christians attempting to form their attitudes and consciences on issues regarding nonviolence and the use of force, pacifism, and military service. But it is also a question that might never even be raised if one were not alert to the concrete social situation of the original human authors and audience of these texts.

Analyzing further, one discovers that at all levels of the NT tradition loving "your enemies" and doing "good to those who persecute you" are understood in the active, even aggressive, sense of a missionary attitude toward enemy and persecutor. It was an appeal to bring enemy and persecutor into the Christian fold (cf. Rom. 12:21).[4] Whether the identification of enemies with persecutors goes back to the historical Jesus cannot be determined. But in any case, the clear meaning of Jesus' teaching, as found in all levels of the NT tradition, is that we should love our enemies, that is, strive to make them our brothers and sisters in the Lord. This gives the love command a public and implicitly political dimension because it explicitly refers to the identity of social groups (cf. Schottroff, 25).

But at this point biblical exegesis leaves us at an impasse, unable to explain how an aggressively active love can be consistent with a passive, nonviolent acceptance of injustice. It seems that we must, as Schottroff suggests, go beyond exegesis to find an answer to this question. We are not going against exegetical evidence, but simply going beyond what exegesis can clearly prove, one way or another, when we see nonresistance in these texts as applying specifically and concretely in the area of politics, especially insurrectional or revolutionary politics. Christians are not revolutionaries, but they do resist evil. The prohibition is not a fundamental rejection of every type of resistance. In fact, as Tertullian put it, Christians are, precisely because they are Christians, factors of resistance in society.[5] They resist injustice, driven by an aggressively missionary love that impels them by nonviolent yet active means to try to bring all, including the persecuting enemy, into the fold of Christ.

If this is so, it relativizes somewhat the NT call to nonviolence and its modern political counterpart, pacifism. It locates the absolute, nonnegotiable center of the Christian message in the positive call to love and not in its negative counterpart and normal mode of realization, nonviolence. This does not imply, for example, that the just-war theory is equally well grounded in the NT as is nonviolence. But it does suggest that one cannot a priori assume that any attempt to

1. cf Lk 7.11-17
2. Egan / T. Avila / Transformation

observe the love command which does not live up to the ideals of nonviolence is necessarily a betrayal of the gospel.

Military Metaphors in the New Testament and Early Church

Adolf von Harnack was the first to point out that military metaphors had a considerable part to play not only in communicating the faith but also in furnishing a model for church life as well.[6] They have a beguiling logic that shapes the minds of all who use them. And since war is a "basic form of life" these metaphors have a universal appeal.[7] All higher religions, Harnack argued, contend for something and against something, and the process of striving can in so many ways find apt parallels in the military life. So in this sense it should be no surprise that early Christianity would make use of these expressions. Yet one can also find irony in that the gospel of peace should be communicated by an implicit contradiction (e.g., "fighting for peace").

Observing the list of military metaphors from the NT, one is immediately aware that none are from the gospels—Jesus apparently did not speak in this way. His preaching is an example of vivid teaching employing seemingly endless metaphors and parables, yet none are drawn from military life. One may conjecture that an explanation of this fact is that Jesus had little contact with military organizations, nor would the people to whom he preached. Of course, he is reported to have talked with a centurion, but still the military action and installations were elsewhere. A likely explanation would be that he sensed the inappropriateness of using that subject to communicate his message.

When we turn to the epistles we find army metaphors used as frequently as any others. There are combat motifs—fighting and struggling—that are general in nature. There are motifs built on weapons, weapons of righteousness, the sword of the spirit. The passage from Ephesians (6:10–18) is the lengthiest and is built up from the equipment for a completely outfitted soldier. Still the terminology is general: it cannot be said that a Roman soldier must have been the only model here even if one cannot imagine what other soldier its author had in mind. Only in Rom. 6:23 do we find a technical term borrowed from the Roman army—*opsōnia*—which was the wages paid to soldiers.

But, since we belong to the day, let us be sober, and put on the breastplate of faith and love, and for a helmet the hope of salvation. (1 Thess. 5:8)

Or is it only Barnabas and I who have no right to refrain from working for a living? Who serves as a soldier at his own expense? Who plants a vineyard without eating any of its fruit? Who tends a flock without getting some of the milk? (1 Cor. 9:6–7)

... but as servants of God we commend ourselves in every way: through great endurance ... with the weapons of righteousness for the right hand and for the left. (2 Cor. 6:4–7)

Do not yield your members to sin as instruments of wickedness, ... and your members to God as instruments of righteousness. (Rom. 6:13)

For the wages [*opsōnia*, military salary] of sin is death, but the free gift of God is eternal life in Christ Jesus our Lord. (Rom. 6:23)

I have thought it necessary to send to you Epaphroditus my brother and fellow worker and fellow soldier. (Phil. 2:25)

To Philemon our beloved fellow worker and Apphia our sister and Archippus our fellow soldier. (Philem. 1–2)

Aristarchus my fellow prisoner [of war] greets you. [The same expression is found in Rom. 16:7 and Philem. 23]. (Col. 4:10)

Finally, be strong in the Lord and in the strength of his might. Put on the whole armor of God, that you may be able to stand against the wiles of the devil. For we are not contending against flesh and blood, but against the principalities, against the powers, against the world rulers of this present darkness, against the spiritual hosts of wickedness in the heavenly places. Therefore take the whole armor of God, that you may be able to withstand in the evil day, and having done all, to stand. Stand therefore, having girded your loins with truth, and having put on the breastplate of righteousness, and having shod your feet with the equipment of the gospel of peace; besides all these, taking the shield of faith, with which you can quench all the flaming darts of the evil one. And take the helmet of salvation, and the sword of the Spirit, which is the word of God. Pray at all times in the Spirit, with all prayer and supplication. To that end keep alert with all perseverance, making supplication for all the saints. (Eph. 6:10–18)

This charge I commit to you, Timothy, my son, in accordance with the prophetic utterances which pointed to you, that inspired by them you may wage the good warfare [fight the good fight]. (1 Tim. 1:18)

Share in suffering as a good soldier of Christ Jesus. No soldier on service gets entangled in civilian pursuits, since his aim is to satisfy the one who enlisted him. An athlete is not crowned unless he competes according to the rules. It is the hard-working farmer who ought to have the first share of the crops. (2 Tim. 2:3–6)

Be faithful unto death, and I will give you the crown of life. (Rev. 2:10)

In the Apostolic Fathers the military metaphors are not nearly as frequent as in the epistles of the NT. Clement of Rome seems to prefer the OT to use as the basis for many of his literary analogies. In the one passage in his first letter to the Corinthians where he makes extended use of an army model, he refers to an army other than that of Rome which had no officers in charge of fifty men.

Let us serve in our army, brethren, with all earnestness, following his faultless commands. Let us consider those who serve our generals, with what good order, habitual readiness, and submissiveness they perform their commands. Not all are prefects, nor tribunes, nor centurions, nor in charge of fifty men [pentēkontarchoi], or the like, but each carries out in his own rank the commands of the emperor and of the generals. (Clement of Rome *First Letter to the Corinthians* 37:1–3)[8]

Clement used the military chain of command as the model for discipline in the church. As such it represents a departure from the uses of these analogies in the NT where they were applied to the individual Christian life. We can see in Clement the beginnings of an extensive system of metaphors which is to burgeon in the years to come; one might go so far as to call it a military theology. In the passage preceding the one cited above, Clement writes about the enemies of God as the ones who "are wicked and oppose his will" (36:6). Consequently it is the church that puts at bay the enemies of God by obeying in the way a soldier obeys his general.

Turning to Ignatius of Antioch we find another analogy which is based partly on the extended Letter of Paul to the Ephesians and partly on his own firsthand experience with the Roman army. Ignatius wrote his epistles while he was traveling under guard to Rome to face trial before the emperor Trajan. The part where he uses Paul's example is in his *Letter to Polycarp* 6.2:

Be pleasing to him in whose ranks you serve, from whom you receive your pay (*opsōnia*)—let none of you be found a deserter. Let your baptism remain as your arms, your faith as a helmet, your love as a spear, your endurance as your panoply, let your works be your deposits (*deposita*) that you may receive the back-pay (*accepta*) due to you. Be therefore longsuffering with one another in gentleness, as God is with you. May I have joy in you always.

As Harnack suggests, Ignatius picked up a military vocabulary from his captors;[9] in fact, Ignatius's Greek has accurately transliterated technical Roman military terms—*desertor, deposita,* and *accepta.* While he has gotten the spirit of Ephesians, he, apparently quoting from memory, misses the letter. Comparing the two passages, one can see that he mismatched the terms; for example, Ephesians has a helmet of salvation whereas Ignatius has a helmet of faith. By comparison Methodius, writing his *Discourse on the Resurrection* more than a century and a half later, got the quotation from Ephesians right (Ante-Nicene Fathers 6:372; abbreviated ANF).

Both Clement and Ignatius are ethically and theologically neutral when they use these metaphors, nor is there any analysis of Christians in a militaristic world. As with the NT, there is not one comment regarding the evil of military life whether the evil be from the morality of combat or from contamination of the idolatrous military religion. For the theme of idolatry we will have to wait for Tertullian to appear on stage.

Should one want to see military metaphors in full bloom, the work of Cyprian is the place to look. Cyprian was a moderate churchman even though he came from North Africa, the land of excess. Cyprian adds new metaphors to the list. A great share of his analogies are focused on comparing the church with the Roman army. Ecclesiology was perhaps Cyprian's greatest interest and this use of metaphors should surprise no one. The church, for example, is the camp:

For this, moreover, is another confession of your faith and praise; to confess that the Church is one, and not to become a sharer in other men's error, or rather wickedness; to seek anew the same camp whence you went forth, whence with the most vigorous strength you leapt forth to the battle to subdue the adversary. For the trophies from the battle-field ought to be brought back thither whence the arms for the field had been received, lest the Church of Christ should not retain those glorious warriors whom Christ had furnished for glory. (Cyprian *Epistle* 50; ANF 5:326)

Just as the Roman army trained its soldiers within the camp, the church also trained the soldiers of Christ (*Epistle* 25; ANF 5:304).

In this same metaphor Cyprian works the analogy from Eph. 6:10–17 (and he gets it right). Christ is the commander of the soldiers (*Epistle* 10; ANF 5:241), and the devil commands the army against them (*On the Exhortation to Martyrdom* 10).

Space does not permit any complete description of Cyprian's military metaphors. It would, however, give the wrong impression to suggest that he used only military models to describe the faith. Cyprian wrote vividly using lots of analogies—one of his favorite subjects was navigation. Frequently, he strung several metaphors together as in the following example from his treatise VII *On the Mortality* (8). The point he makes is that all men share the fact of mortality.

Thus, when the earth is barren with an unproductive harvest, famine makes no distinction; thus, when with the invasion of an enemy any city is taken, captivity at once desolates all; and when the serene clouds withhold the rain, the drought is alike to all; and when the rocks rend the ship the shipwreck is common without exception to all that sail in her.

It is clear that these metaphors had a compelling logic that, as Harnack suggested, appeared time and again in many of the writers of the early church and later. He may well be correct in suggesting that the use of these metaphors was a contributing factor in shaping the mind of the church when it contemplated the morality of war, that the army of Christ became the actual armies of the medieval church.

NOTES

1. In this we are particularly indebted to L. Schottroff, "Non-Violence and the Love of One's Enemies," in *Essays on the Love Commandment*, trans. R. H. Fuller and I. Fuller (Philadelphia: Fortress Press, 1978), 9–39, particularly as used in R. Daly, "Love and Non-Violence in the New Testament and Early Church," in *Non-Violence—Central to Christian Spirituality: Perspectives from Scripture to the Present*, ed. J. Culliton (Toronto: Edwin Mellen, 1982), 33–62.

2. Cf. R. A. Edwards, *A Theology of Q: Eschatology, Prophecy and Wisdom* (Philadelphia: Fortress Press, 1976), 25, 32–43, 58–79, and H. C. Kee, *Jesus in History* (New York: Harcourt Brace Jovanovich, 1970), 62–103.

3. Cf. H. Schürmann, *Das Lukasevangelium* I, HTKNT 3 (Freiburg and Vienna: Herder, 1969), 344, 349, as cited by Schottroff, "Non-Violence," 12.

4. Schottroff, "Non-Violence," 23. We can only conjecture how effectively or actively Christians did this, nor can we do much more than conjecture what causal factor aggressive conversion tactics may have played in the persecutions.

5. Tertullian *Apology* 37; cf. Schottroff, "Non-Violence," 27.

6. Adolf von Harnack, *Militia Christi: The Christian Religion and the Military in the First Three Centuries*, trans. D. Gracie (Philadelphia: Fortress Press, 1981), 27–64.

7. Harnack, *Militia Christi*, 27.

8. Trans. Kirsopp Lake, LCL, 1912.

9. Harnack, *Militia Christi*, 41.

3.

Tertullian

Tertullian is the first Christian writer to give extensive attention to this theme. We will consider the evidence from his writings in two parts. The first part consists of his *Apology* and the *Treatise on Idolatry*. The second part is his work devoted principally to the nature of Roman army religion and the Christian's place in it, the *Treatise on the Crown*. It is assumed by most, though not conclusively proven, that this latter work was from Tertullian's later years as one of the Montanists. But, as we will show, Tertullian maintained throughout his writings a consistent view of the inadvisability of Christians entering the Roman army.

Tertullian's *Apology*, addressed to the emperor Septimius Severus in the year 197, contains the understanding that war is necessary, although he decried the killing and destruction it leaves behind (*Apology* 25.14). He could not deny the legitimate power of the state because the emperor came to power by the pleasure of God and, therefore, Christians pray for him and for brave armies as well:

Without ceasing, for all our emperors we offer prayer. We pray for life prolonged; for security to the empire; for protection to the imperial house; for brave armies, a faithful senate, a virtuous people, the world at rest, whatever, as man or Caesar, an emperor would wish. (*Apology* 30.4; ANF 3:42)

In fact, Tertullian could not envision a future that did not include the empire as a tool in God's plan for shaping the future. As one might expect in an apology for the legitimacy of Christians in the empire, Tertullian repeatedly argued that Christians were loyal to Rome. It must be assumed that Romans had made the charge that Christians had refused to enter the military; but we have no evidence that Tertullian read Celsus who made that exact complaint. By way of refuting those accusations, Tertullian pointed out that there were Christians in every military camp who, along with a host of other endeavors, fought in the army as well. He even toys with one of the

Romans' chief fears, that of revolution and insurrection. He points out that, were they of a mind to do so, the Christians could cause a lot of trouble for the empire. Fortunately for Rome, Christians think it "better to be slain than to slay."

Yet, banded together as we are, ever so ready to sacrifice our lives, what single case of revenge for injury are you able to point to, though, if it were held right among us to repay evil by evil, a single night with a torch or two could achieve an ample vengeance . . . If we desired, indeed, to act the part of open avengers, would there be any lacking in strength, whether of numbers or resources? . . . We are but of yesterday, and we have filled every place among you—cities, islands, fortresses, towns, market-places, the very camp, tribes, companies, palace, senate, forum—we have left nothing to you but the temples of your gods. For what wars should we not be fit, not eager, even with unequal forces, we who so willingly yield ourselves to the sword, if in our religion it were not counted better to be slain than to slay? (*Apology* 37.3)

Obviously the context of this last sentence has to do with the loyalty of Christians to Rome and nothing to do with any policy of Christians enlisting or fighting in military combat. In no way does Tertullian apologize to anyone that Christians are involved in the same pursuits as are every other Roman.

So we sojourn with you in the world abjuring neither forum, nor shambles, nor bath, nor booth, nor workshop, nor inn, nor weekly market, nor any other places of commerce. We sail with you, and fight with you, and till the ground with you; and in like manner we unite with you in your traffickings—even in the various arts we make public property of our works for your benefit. (*Apology* 42.2–3)

In making these statements, Tertullian, among other things, had in mind the story of the Thundering Legion (see chap. 4 below) which had Christians in it who were of decisive help in that victory. It is important to note that, in those contexts where he was protesting the loyalty of Christians, Tertullian never bothered to qualify his statements.

It can never be said, however, that Tertullian had no misgivings about Christian participation in the army. Already in the *Apology* we catch a faint glimpse of what, in a decade or two, will grow into a major theme: that the military standards of the camp are idolatrous because they are worshiped above all other gods (*Apology* 16.8). Fourteen years later in his *Treatise on Idolatry* he put it this way:

But now the question is whether a believer can become a soldier and whether a soldier can be admitted into the faith, even if he is a member only of the rank and file who are not required to take part in sacrifices or capital punishments.

There can be no compatibility between the divine and the human sacrament (= military oath), the standard of Christ and the standard of the devil, the camp of light and the camp of darkness. One soul cannot serve two masters—God and Caesar. Moses, to be sure, carried a rod; Aaron wore a military belt, and John (the Baptist) is girt with leather (i.e., like a soldier); and, if you really want to play around with the subject, Joshua the son of Nun led an army and the people waged war. But how will a Christian man go to war? Indeed how will he serve even in peacetime without a sword which the Lord has taken away? For even if soldiers came to John and received advice on how to act, and even if a centurion became a believer, the Lord, in subsequently disarming Peter, disarmed every soldier. No uniform is lawful among us if it is designated for an unlawful action. (*Treatise on Idolatry* 19; ANF 3:73)

This quotation sums up Tertullian's major objection to Christians serving in the military; from this position he never wavered. For him the military life was one set in total opposition to the Christian life, and one had to choose one or the other. Some scholars, such as Roland Bainton,[2] have minimized the power and extent of Roman army religion, but in our view such a perspective overlooks much recent evidence showing how the army was a religious system, a "total institution" (see chap. 8 below).

It is indeed interesting that Tertullian would discuss the topic of military service in the treatise concerning idolatry. This points out that the question of military service was offensive to him primarily in that context. As Tertullian saw it, the idolatry of the military forced Christians into two offenses against the faith: taking part in sacrifices and executing capital sentences. Nothing is said about combat. That is why Tertullian seems to be as concerned with the question of whether a soldier could serve in peacetime. We will encounter this same problem when we deal with canon III of the Synod of Arles which stipulates that soldiers are not to throw down their arms in a time of *peace*, not war (see below at the end of chap. 10). And finally, it seems clear that Tertullian knew that the belt and uniform of the soldier were regarded as symbolic, both for the Roman authorities and the Christians who objected to them.

It is difficult to read Tertullian's *Treatise on the Crown* and not sense the impression military religion had made on his mind. The occasion for this treatise was the martyrdom of a Christian soldier who refused to conform to the uniform (dress) requirements for a military ceremony. For the reception of a donative, a bonus granted by the emperor, the soldiers were to present themselves in full military parade dress, including a military crown. This particular anonymous soldier refused to wear his crown, instead carrying it in his hand. Since the soldier was out of uniform he was arrested and, presumably, executed. Tertullian tells us that there were other Christian soldiers in that detachment for he rebuked those brothers of the martyr who "presumed to serve two lords." He also called them "laurel-crowned Christians" (1.6). From the beginning to the end of the treatise, Tertullian's argument revolves around the unacceptability of joining the Roman army because of its idolatrous nature. In the first section of the treatise (1.6—7.2) he adopted the arguments from Stoicism that wearing a crown is unnatural because one cannot smell flowers on the top of one's head. The crown is idolatrous because it is *contra naturam*. The second section (7.3—11.3) connects the use of the crown with various cults and deities of Greek and Roman society. From this perspective, too, the crown is idolatrous.

It is in the last chapter (11) of this section that Tertullian focuses again on the Roman military. It is because of the idolatrous nature of the army that military life is evil; the structure of his argument shows that he saw evil proceeding from idolatry. "What sense is there in discussing the merely accidental [i.e., military life], when that on which it rests [the idolatrous crown] is to be condemned?" To demonstrate the power of idolatry, Tertullian mentions everything that he found objectionable as examples of that power—the military oath, the use of the sword, guard duties involving torture and securing pagan sanctuaries, the flag, trumpets, and cremation. Even though he knew of centurions from the NT who served without stigma, he concluded that no Christian could remain in the service after baptism. Army religion was simply so corrosive that he felt none could withstand its effects—just like the Christians who (in the first chapter of the treatise) had given in to it.

Tertullian's knowledge of what went on inside the walls of the army camp shows evidence of being well informed on its details. It appears that he was close to a camp or had gotten the information from some reliable source, perhaps a veteran. Jerome thought that he must have been the son of a centurion.[3] There is, however, no internal evidence in any of Tertullian's writings to substantiate this point. Of all the church fathers, Tertullian shows that he is the one most acquainted with the army and particularly its ceremonies and rituals. He has assessed correctly the Roman army as a religious institution that covered nearly every aspect of the soldiers' life under arms. Of course, he knows that Jesus would not have been in the military. The statement that "those who live by the sword shall perish by the sword" is directed against the less conscientious comrades of those soldiers who refused the military crown. Presumably these, along with many others, stayed in the army, living two lives as Tertullian saw it. They stood guard on the Sabbath and over Roman temples that he would have exorcized. Tertullian objected to the legionary standards and the insignia on the uniforms of the soldiers that the Romans believed were the chief radiators of religious power to the legions. Many Christians had gone into the legions and consequently lost their faith. Others had to resort to compromises with both Christian and military requirements.

The *Treatise on the Crown* is thoroughly a statement on the dangers of idolatry. In this sense, it is an extension of his earlier *Treatise on Idolatry*. In a word, idolatry was one of Tertullian's foremost functional ideas when he reflected about the relationship between the church and its environment. The *Treatise on the Crown,* even though it begins with recounting an incident in the military and returns here and there to idolatry in military life, is a discussion about idolatry generally. Although G. de Plinval is not correct when he describes it as a diatribe against Mithraism, he is on the right track in identifying it as a document involving religious, not ethical, conflicts.[4]

Only at the end in chapter 15 does the explicit reference to Mithraism appear. In writing this, Tertullian is one of very few literary witnesses to Mithraism, especially its initiation rites. Why does Tertullian say that Mithraism attempted to copy Christianity? The answer to this question reveals an underlying issue in the study of the relationship between Christianity and the Roman army. No soldier, we may be safe in saying, was an astute theologian; and we cannot be surprised if there was confusion between the two religious communities. So Tertullian was trying, as best he could, to draw some boundaries between them. Perhaps many soldiers repeatedly crossed those boundaries. It would have been standard Roman practice for them to do so. If we back away from the entire treatise, it makes a good deal of sense to see the purpose of this work and many others of Tertullian (cf. *On Idolatry*) as attempts to keep the Christian religion from being diluted into nonexistence in a pluralistic Roman world.

TREATISE ON THE CROWN

Chapter 1

Very lately it happened thus: while the bounty of our most excellent emperors was dispensed in the camp, the soldiers, laurel-crowned, were approaching. One of them, more a soldier of God, more steadfast than the rest of his brethren, who had imagined that they could serve two masters, his head alone uncovered, the useless crown in his hand—already even by that peculiarity known to every one as a Christian—was nobly conspicuous. Accordingly, all began to mark him out, jeering him at a distance, gnashing on him near at hand. The murmur is wafted to the tribune, when the person had just left the ranks. The tribune at once puts the question to him, Why are you so different in your attire? He declared that he had no liberty to wear the crown with the rest. Being urgently asked for his reasons, he answered, I am a Christian. O soldier! boasting thyself in God. Then the case was considered and voted on; the matter was remitted to a higher tribunal; the offender was conducted to the prefects. At once he put away the heavy cloak, his disburdening commenced; he loosed from his foot the military shoe, beginning to stand upon holy ground; he gave up the sword, which was not necessary either for the protection of our Lord; from his hand likewise dropped the laurel crown; and now, purple-clad with the hope of his own blood, shod with the preparation of the gospel, girt with the sharper word of God, completely equipped in the apostles' armor, and crowned more worthily with the crown of martyrdom, he awaits in prison the donative of Christ. Thereafter adverse judgments began to be passed upon his conduct—whether on the part of Christians I do not know, for those of the heathen are not different—as if he were headstrong and rash, and too eager to die, because in being taken to task about a mere matter of dress, he brought trouble on the bearers of the Name—he, forsooth, alone brave among so many soldier-brethren, he alone a Christian. It is plain that as they have rejected the prophecies of the Holy Spirit, they are also purposing the refusal of martyrdom. So they murmur that a peace so good and long is endangered for them. Nor do I doubt that some are already turning their back on the Scriptures, are making ready their luggage, are equipped for flight from city to city; for that is all of the gospel they care to remember. I know, too, their pastors are lions in peace, deer in the fight. As to the questions asked for extorting confessions from us, we shall teach elsewhere. Now, as they put forth also the objection—But where are we forbidden to be crowned?—I shall take this point up, as more suitable to be treated of here, being the essence, in fact, of the present contention. So that, on the one hand, the inquirers who are ignorant, but anxious, may be instructed; and on the other, those may be refuted who try to vindicate the sin, especially the laurel-crowned Christians themselves, to whom it is merely a question of debate, as if it might be regarded as either no trespass at all, or at least a doubtful one, because it may be made the subject of investigation. That it is neither sinless nor doubtful, I shall now, however, show.

Chapter 11

To begin with the real ground of the military crown, I think we must first inquire whether military service is proper at all for Christians [*an in totum Christianis militia conueniat*]. What sense is there in discussing the merely accidental, when that on which it rests is to be condemned? Do we believe it lawful for a human oath to be superadded to one divine, for a man to come under promise to another master after Christ, and to abjure father, mother, and all nearest kinsfolk, whom even the law has commanded us to honor and love next to God himself, to whom the gospel, too, holding them only of less account than Christ, has in like manner rendered honor? Shall it be held lawful to make an occupation of the sword, when the Lord proclaims that he who uses the sword shall perish by the sword? And shall the son of peace take part in the battle when it does not become him even to sue at law? And shall he apply the chain, and the prison, and the torture, and the punishment, who is not the avenger even of his own wrongs? Shall he, forsooth, either keep watch-service for others more than for Christ, or shall he do it on the Lord's day, when he does not even do it for Christ Himself? And shall he keep guard before the temples which he has renounced? And shall he take a meal where the apostle has forbidden him? And shall he diligently protect by night those whom in the day-time he has put to flight by his exorcisms, leaning and resting on the spear the while with which Christ's side was pierced? Shall he carry a flag, too, hostile to Christ? And shall *he* ask a watchword from the emperor who has already received one from God? Shall *he* be disturbed in death by the trumpet of the trumpeter, who expects to be aroused by the angel's trump? And shall the Christian be burned according to camp rule, when he was not permitted to burn incense to an idol, when to him Christ remitted the punishment of fire? Then how many other offences there are involved in the performances of camp offices, which we must hold to involve a transgression of God's law, you may see by a slight survey. The very carrying of the name over from the camp of light to the camp of darkness is a violation of it. Of course, if faith comes later, and finds any already occupied with military service, their case is different, as in the instance of those whom John used to receive for baptism, and of those most faithful centurions, I mean the centurion whom Christ approves, and the centurion whom Peter instructs; yet, at the same time, when a man has become a believer, and faith has been sealed, there must be either an immediate abandonment of it, which has been the course with many; or all sorts of quibbling will have to be resorted to in order to avoid offending God, and that is not allowed even outside of military service; or, last of all, for God the fate must be endured which a citizen-faith has been no less ready to accept. Neither does military service hold out escape from punishment of sins, or exemption from martyrdom. Nowhere does the Christian change his character. There is one gospel, and the same Jesus, who will one day deny every one who denies, and acknowledge every one who acknowledges God—who will save, too, the life which has been lost for His sake; but, on the other hand, destroy that which for gain has been saved to His dishonor. With Him the faithful citizen is a soldier, just as the faithful soldier is a citizen. A state of faith admits no plea of necessity; they are under no necessity to sin, whose one necessity is, that they do not sin. For if one is pressed to the offering of sacrifice and the sheer denial of Christ by the necessity of torture or of punishment, yet discipline does not connive even at that necessity; because there is a higher necessity to dread denying and to undergo martyrdom, than to escape from suffering, and to render the homage required. In fact, an excuse of this sort overturns the entire essence of our sacrament, removing even the obstacle to voluntary sins; for it will be possible also to maintain that inclination is a necessity, as involving in it, forsooth, a sort of compulsion. I have, in fact, disposed of this very allegation of necessity with reference to the pleas by which crowns connected with official position are vindicated, in support of which it is in common use, since for this very reason offices must be either refused, that we may not fall into acts of sin, or martyrdoms endured that we may get quit of offices. Touching this primary aspect of the question, as to the unlawfulness even of military life itself, I shall not add more, that the secondary question may be restored to its place. Indeed, if putting my strength to the question, I banish from us the military life, I should now to no purpose issue a challenge on the matter of the military crown. Suppose, then, that the military service is lawful, as far as the plea for the crown is concerned.

Chapter 12

But I first say a word about the crown itself. This laurel one is sacred to Apollo or Bacchus—to the former as the god of archery, to the latter as the god of triumphs. In like manner Claudius teaches, when he tells us that soldiers are wont too to be wreathed in myrtle. For the myrtle belongs to Venus, the mother of the Aeneadae, the mistress also of the god of war, who through the Ilia and the Romuli is Roman. But I do not believe that Venus is Roman as well as Mars, because of the vexation the concubine gave her. When military service again is crowned with olive, the idolatry has respect to Minerva, who is equally the goddess of arms—but got a crown of the tree referred to, because of the peace she made with Neptune. In these respects, the superstition of the military garland will be everywhere defiled and all-defiling. And it is further defiled, I should think, also in the grounds of it. Lo! the yearly public pronouncing of vows, what does that bear on its face to be? It takes place first in the part of the camp where the general's tent is, and then in the temples. In addition to the places, observe the words also: "We vow that you, O Jupiter, will then have an ox with gold-decorated horns." What does the utterance mean? Without a doubt the denial (of Christ). Albeit the Christian says nothing in these places with the mouth, he makes his response by having the crown on his head. The laurel is likewise commanded (to be used) at the distribution of the donative. So you see idolatry is not without its gain, selling, as it does, Christ for pieces of gold, as Judas did for pieces of silver. Will it be "You cannot serve God and mammon," to devote your energies to mammon, and to depart from God? Will it be "Render unto Caesar the things which are Caesar's, and unto God the things which are God's," not only to render the human being to God, but even to take the denarius from Caesar? Is the laurel of the triumph made of leaves, or of corpses? Is it adorned with ribbons, or with tombs? Is it bedewed with ointments, or with the tears of wives and mothers? It may be of some Christians too; for Christ is also among the barbarians. Has not he who has carried (a crown for) this cause on his head, fought even against himself? Another sort of service belongs to the royal guards. And indeed crowns are called *Castrenses,* as belonging to the camp; *Munificae* likewise, from the Caesarian functions they perform. But even then you are still the soldier and the servant of another; and of the two masters, of God and Caesar; but assuredly then not of Caesar, when you owe yourself to God, as having higher claims, I should think, even in matters in which both have an interest.

Chapter 15

Keep for God His own property untainted; He will crown it if He choose. Nay, then, He does even choose. He calls us to it. To him who conquers He says, "I will give a crown of life." Be *you,* too, faithful unto death, and fight *you* too, the good fight, whose crown the apostle feels so justly confident has been laid up for him. The angel also, as he goes forth on a white horse, conquering and to conquer, receives a crown of victory; and another is adorned with an encircling rainbow (as it were in its fair colors)—a celestial meadow. In like manner, the elders sit crowned around, crowned too with a crown of gold, and the Son of Man Himself flashes out above the clouds. If such are the appearances in the vision of the seer, of what sort will be the realities in the actual manifestation? Look at those crowns. Inhale those odors. Why condemn you to a little chaplet, or a twisted headband, the brow of which has been destined for a diadem? For Christ Jesus has made us even kings to God and His Father. What have you in common with the flower which is to die? You have a flower in the Branch of Jesse, upon which the grace of the Divine Spirit in all its fulness rested—a flower undefiled, unfading, everlasting, by choosing which the good soldier, too, has got promotion in the heavenly ranks. Blush, you fellow-soldiers of his, henceforth not to be condemned even by him, but by some soldier of Mithras, who, at his initiation in the gloomy cavern, in the camp, it may well be said, of darkness, when at the sword's point a crown is presented to him, as though in mimicry of martyrdom, and thereupon put upon his head, is admonished to resist and cast it off, and, if you like, transfer it to his shoulder, saying that Mithras is his crown. And thenceforth he is never crowned; and he has that for a mark to show who he is, if anywhere he is subjected to trial in respect of his religion; and he is at once believed to be a soldier of Mithras if he throws the crown away—if he says that in his god he has his crown. Let us take note of the devices of the devil, who is wont to ape some of God's things with no other design than, by the faithfulness of his servants, to put us to shame, and to condemn us.

In conclusion, what should be said about the position that holds that Tertullian was a pacifist? First, a few statements about regretting killing in connection with the army do not add up to a pacifist stance. Some of the most ruthless generals have been known to make such statements. Nowhere are these developed into an argument of any kind. In all the hundreds of pages of Tertullian's work one cannot find even one whole paragraph devoted to that topic. In view of the (to us) recondite topics he developed, it would seem that if he thought at all about pacifism he would presumably have written a great deal about it. Second, nowhere is there any statement that a soldier should not enlist because killing in combat is wrong. It would seem that one such statement, if not many, would be a necessary condition for establishing in Tertullian's theology a principle of Christian pacifism. Third, statements such as "Christians would rather be killed than kill" have to be seen in their wider contexts in order to see that they were not uttered in any context dealing with the military (*Apology* 37.5); to use them to build or support a theory of Christian pacifism is totally irresponsible to the text.

NOTES

1. This section on Tertullian is basically a summary of the more thorough statement of J. Helgeland, "Christians and the Roman Army from Marcus Aurelius to Constantine," *Aufstieg und Niedergang der römischen Welt* 2.23.1, ed. W. Haase (Berlin, 1979), 724–44, here 735–44 (abbreviated *ANRW*).

2. Roland Bainton, *Christian Attitudes toward War and Peace* (Nashville and New York: Abingdon Press, 1960).

3. *De viribus illustribus* 53.

4. G. de Plinval, "Tertullian et le scandale de la couronne," *Mélanges Joseph de Ghellinck S.J.* (Gembloux: J. Duculot, 1951) 1:183–88.

4.

The Thundering Legion

Eusebius tells the fascinating story of the *Legio XII Fulminata,* the Thundering Legion, that was credited with decisively aiding Marcus Aurelius in the year 173. This legion was fighting the Germans and the Sarmatians on the Danube frontier when it got trapped and was kept from food and water. The soldiers were dangerously weakened from thirst and unable to hold out much longer when Christians in the legion prayed for deliverance. Immediately a rainstorm blew up that filled the Roman water barrels and put the enemy to flight with bolts of lightning. The Romans had only to mop up. This is how Eusebius tells the story:

Such were the events which happened under Antoninus.

It is said that when his brother, Marcus Aurelius Caesar, was engaging in battle with the Germans and Sarmatians, he was in difficulties, because his army was oppressed by thirst; but the soldiers of the legion which is called after Melitene [in eastern Cappadocia], knelt on the ground according to our own custom of prayer, in the faith which has sustained them from that time to this in their contests with their enemies, and turned towards God with supplications. Now though this kind of spectacle seemed strange to the enemy, the story goes that another still more marvellous overcame them at once, for lightning drove the enemy to flight and destruction, and a shower falling on the army which had prayed to God, refreshed them all when they were on the point of destruction from thirst.

The story is both told among writers who are foreign to our faith who have undertaken to write of the times of the above mentioned emperors, and has also been recorded by Christians. By the heathen writers, inasmuch as they were strangers to the faith, the miracle is related, but it was not confessed that it happened through the prayers of the Christians; but in our own writers, inasmuch as they are the friends of truth, what happened has been described in a simple and harmless fashion. Among these would be also Apolinarius, who states that after that time the legion which had wrought the miracle through prayer had received a name from the emperor appropriate to what had happened, and was called in Latin the "Thundering Legion." Tertullian is also a worthy witness of these things, who in addressing in Latin an apology for our faith to the Senate, which we have quoted already, confirmed the story with more and clearer proof. In his writing he says that letters of Marcus, the most prudent emperor, were still extant, in which he testifies himself that when his army was on the point of destruction in Germany from lack of water it had been saved by the prayers of the Christians, and Tertullian says that the emperor also threatened death to those who attempted to accuse us. The author goes on as follows: "What kind of laws are these which wicked, unrighteous, and cruel men use against us alone? Vespasian did not observe them although he conquered the Jews. Trajan partially allowed them, but forbade Christians to be sought out. Neither Hadrian, though busy in all curious matters, nor Pius, as he is called, ratified them." But let these things be as anyone will, we must pass on to the train of further events. (Eusebius *Ecclesiastical History* V.4.3–5.7)

It might be easy to cast this story aside were it not reported by non-Christian sources as well. Cassius Dio tells it in his history at even greater length (Dio LXXXII, 8.1—10.5). In Dio, however, the deliverance came not through intervention of the Christians' God but at the hands of an Egyptian magician, Arnuphus, who was traveling in the entourage of Marcus. Dio also states that the fortuitous outcome led the Senate to proclaim Marcus *Imperator* for the seventh time and his wife Faustina became acclaimed the "Mother of the Camp."[1] In the eleventh century a Christian historian, Johannes Xiphilinus, interpreted Dio's account denying the effect of Egyptian magic. Xiphilinus tells us that on account of the victory, Marcus wrote a dispatch to the Senate giving credit to the Christians for that victory and that in the honor of the Christians he gave the twelfth legion the title of "Thundering."

The interpolation is hard to believe for several reasons. Sources contemporary with Marcus know nothing about such a letter. The supposed change in Marcus's attitude must, in any case, have been short-lived because he gave permission for the bloody persecution of Christians in Lyons-Vienne only four years later. Eusebius reported the persecution but, by way of apologetics, tried to pass it off on Marcus's half brother Verus who had been dead for eight years. Marcus's attitude to the Christians can be read from his *Meditations* (III, 16) where he said that the Christians had failed the empire "in its time of need." There is a problem, too, with the title "thundering." *Fulminata* is a perfect passive participle best translated "thunderstruck" not "thundering" which is a present active participle. Obviously, the camp had been struck by lightning long ago; an important omen. The title *Fulminata* goes back to the reign of Augustus, which covered the years 28 B.C.E. to 14 C.E., so that anachronism proves Xiphilinus wrong.[2]

Despite Xiphilinus's meddling with the text there is solid reason to believe that the accounts of Eusebius and Dio contain authentic elements. The column of Marcus in Rome, erected in 176, has scenes depicting his career, three of which describe the event of the rainstorm.[3] Here the thunderbolt is credited to the prayers of Marcus himself shown on bended knee. The rainstorm, however, is the work of Juppiter Pluvius, Juppiter acting as a rain god with water pouring down from his outstretched arms.

What we have seen in these various accounts is an ideological battle expressed in religious symbolism. Everyone wanted to have his deity receive credit for the victory that undoubtedly involved rain and lightning. Even Tertullian got into the act; he claimed the victory as evidence that the Christians had always been loyal to the empire and that their loyalty indeed had positive consequences for the empire (*Apology* 5). None of the Christian writers, not Apolinarius, not Eusebius, not Tertullian regretted that Christians were involved with the victory. All recounted the incident with pride.

So how much were Christians involved? First of all, no Roman source stated that the *XII Fulminata* was present at the battle, nor does any such source tell us about the names of any legion there. The Thundering Legion had quartered in the camp at Melitene ever since it was nearly destroyed by the Jews in the year 66 at the beginning of the Jewish War. The legion even lost its eagle but was not disbanded because all its defenders had been wiped out.[4] Melitene, located in Cappadocia in modern eastern Turkey, was a long way from the Danube. Yet we know that Marcus assembled his army by pulling contingents from legions in Europe and North Africa. We also know that the legion was instrumental in putting down the revolt of Avidius Cassius who was in fact assassinated in the camp of the *XII Fulminata* for which the legion received the honor of being called *certa constans* ("always dependable"). The year was 175, less than two years after the rainstorm. Most likely, the legion was there all along, but had sent part of its membership along to help Marcus on the Danube.

Why can we say there were Christians in the legion? Apolinarius lived close to the camp at that time. We remember he was the first to tell the story of the rainstorm. Then too, Trajan had raised the town to the level of a *municipium* thereby conferring upon the residents Roman citizenship. It was necessary to have citizenship in order to enlist in a legion. And, finally, we know that the population in that neighborhood was highly Christian at that time. For Apolinarius to pass the story along it had to have the ring of authenticity—it fits what we know of the facts.

More than likely, Christians had been enlisting in this legion, and others as well, for some time. Even though the incident of the rainstorm is the first evidence of Christian involvement in the Roman military, there is no good reason to assume that these were the first Christian soldiers. Their number increased steadily until the time of Diocletian when they were a large enough number to attract imperial notice. He had to prepare for his persecution in the year 303 by first purging the army of Christians.

NOTES

1. *Feriale Duranum* festival of 20 September; *C.I.L.* 14.40.
2. E. Ritterling, "Legio," *Real-Encyclopädie der klassischen Alter-tumswissenschaft*, ed. Pauly-Wissowa (Stuttgart: J.B. Metzler, 1925), 12.1186–1829; *C.I.L.* 3.504, 507, 509, 6097; 5.2520; 9.435.
3. Giovanni Becatti, *Colonna di Marco Aurelio* (Milan: Editoriale Domus, 1957), plates 9, 10, 11, 12.
4. John Helgeland, "Roman Army Religion," *ANRW* 2.16.2, pp. 1475–76.

5.

Hippolytus

When it comes to Hippolytus we are, for several reasons, on unsure footing. There is some question as to whether the text of his *Apostolic Tradition* is reliably ascribed to him or whether the form in which it has come down to us is accurate.[1] Even if we take the text at face value there is a further problem of deciding who it is that Hippolytus represents. A rigorist, he eventually withdrew from the Roman church and became a so-called antipope. Some of his other works show that he was attracted by Jewish thought, particularly that of the Essenes, and that he had more knowledge of it than might be expected of a Roman. The Essenes had vanished a century and a half before, yet his church order has vestigial traces of Jewish models.[2] His work betrays a thoroughgoing revulsion toward the Roman state and its idolatrous practices. In this attitude he joins Tertullian, another rigorist, but without showing influences of Montanism which captivated the mind of the African churchman.[3] Thus the large question, which space does not allow us to address here, is whether Hippolytus speaks for himself or for the consensus of the church at Rome or elsewhere.

With these reservations in mind we turn to an examination of the portion of the *Apostolic Tradition* where he deals with some occupations Christians might pursue. If one assumes that Hippolytus did not go to the trouble of issuing prohibitions against what was not actually taking place, it appears that Christians were involved with a wide range of occupations, some of them quite shady. There seem to be two criteria on which Hippolytus bases his objections to various occupations: personal immorality and idolatry.

Articles 14 and 15 refer to gladiators in the games. Such activity was morally offensive to Christians as well as to the more sensitive in the empire such as Seneca; mass killing for the sake of spectacle is well known. Less well known, however, is the religious aspect of the shows, which Hippolytus certainly would have regarded as idolatry. Tertullian did. His treatise *On the Shows,* chapter 4, connects the wanton killing with idolatry at every point. Idolatry, moreover, is "the crowning sin" (chapter 2) from which stems every other moral outrage in the games. The games frequently took place in connection with funerals such as the one Julius Caesar produced for his father—involving 640 gladiators and condemned criminals. Although the Romans abhorred human sacrifice in foreign religions, the Druids for example, they practiced it wholesale in the games expressing motifs of shedding blood for the dead.[4] Not only did the shows involve the gods Mars and Mercury, but Tertullian regarded the whole practice as a pollution. Particularly offensive was the connection of the games with war; in peacetime the Romans kept up the martial spirit by means of the murderous shows, murderous because the justification of self-defense was totally absent. In Tertullian's mind, and most likely for Hippolytus as well, all this was the consequence of idolatry.

Articles 17–19 of the *Apostolic Tradition* put the occupation of the military in the same context of idolatry. The reference to execution (article 17) could suggest the killing of criminals in connection with the gladiatorial events, persecution, or simply capital punishment. It seems clear that the train of thought before and after rules out the taking of life in combat as its meaning. Speaking of a soldier in authority is interesting, too, for the suggestion that there are some Christian soldiers who have risen up in the ranks. This is, of course, no surprise in that, if a Christian were in the army, he like any other soldier would be serious about it and take his normal promotions. Telling a soldier not to take the military oath (*sacramentum*) might seem nonsensical: a civilian becomes a soldier by means of taking the military oath. Yet, as we show elsewhere, the recital of the military oath was a regularly repeated feature of army life, one which took place at least three times annually; one would even be correct in calling it a liturgical practice. Articles 18 and 19 add nothing substantially to what has already been said in explanation of article 17. They merely point out by implication that Christians aspired to these positions and that some of these positions may have been prestigious. Enlisting is just another way in which one might have committed adultery, namely, despising God. The remainder of the portion quoted from the *Apostolic Tradition* merely continues the train of thought concerning individual immorality and idolatry.

The detail with which we inspect this passage is justified by the weight some interpreters place on it in an attempt to establish an early

Christian pacifism. As we have seen, nothing of the sort is indicated. There is no reference whatever to a prohibition of killing in combat whether in defense of or in expansion of the empire, though the latter did attract criticism by people like Tertullian who objected to war as a means of aggrandizing Rome. To put this passage further in perspective, it is the only place in all of Hippolytus's extant work where he mentions the topic of military service, an obvious indication of the apparently small importance he gave it.

THE APOSTOLIC TRADITION[5]

[Of the crafts and professions (*forbidden to Christians*)]

9. [*They shall enquire about the crafts and occupations of those who are brought for instruction.*]

Immoral

10. If a man be a pander who supports harlots either let him desist or let him be rejected.

11. If a man be a sculptor or a painter, he shall be taught not to make idols. If he will not desist, let him be rejected.

12. If a man be an actor or one who makes shows in the theatre, either let him desist or let him be rejected.

Schoolmaster

13. If a man teach children worldly knowledge, it is indeed well if he desist. But if he has no other trade by which to live, let him have forgiveness.

Circus

14. A charioteer likewise [or one who takes part in the games or who goes to the games], either let him desist or let him be rejected.

Amphitheatre

15. A man who is a gladiator or a trainer of gladiators or a huntsman [in the arena] or one concerned with wild-beast shows or a public official who is concerned with gladiatorial shows, either let him desist or let him be rejected.

Idolatry

16. If a man be a priest of idols or a keeper of idols, either let him desist or let him be rejected.

Servants of the Pagan State

17. A soldier who is in authority must be told not to execute men; if he should be ordered to do it, he shall not do it. He must be told not to take the military oath. If he will not agree, let him be rejected.

18. A military governor or a magistrate of a city who wears the purple, either let him desist or let him be rejected.

19. If a catechumen or a baptised Christian wishes to become a soldier [i.e., *a volunteer*] let him be cast out. For he has despised God.

Immorality

20. A harlot or a sodomite [*or one who has castrated himself*] or one who does things which may not be spoken of, let them be rejected for they are defiled.

Magic

21. A magician shall not even be brought for consideration.

22. A charmer or an astrologer or an interpreter of dreams or a mountebank [or a clipper of fringes of clothes] or a maker of amulets, let them desist or let them be rejected.

Concubinage

23. If a man's concubine be a slave, let her hear on condition that she have reared her children, and if she consorts with him alone. But if not let her be rejected.

24a. If a man have a concubine, let him desist and marry legally; and if he will not, let him be rejected.

24b. [*And if a baptised woman consort with a slave, either let her desist or let her be rejected.*]

25. [*If we have omitted anything, decide ye as is fit; for we all have the Spirit of God.*]

NOTES

1. Jacques Fontaine, "Christians and Military Service in the Early Church," *Concilium* 7 (1965): 58–64.

2. W. H. C. Frend, *Martyrdom and Persecution in the Early Church* (Garden City, N.Y.: Doubleday Anchor Books, 1967), 280.

3. R. M. Grant, *Augustus to Constantine* (New York: Harper & Row, 1970), 183.

4. Keith Hopkins, "Murderous Games," *History Today* 33 (June 1983): 16–22, here 17.

5. Gregory Dix and Rev. H. Chadwick, eds., *The Treatise on the Apostolic Tradition of St. Hippolytus of Rome* (London: SPCK, 1968), 24–28.

6.

Origen

Origen (ca. 185–251?), possibly the most important of the early church writers,[1] has been described as "the most articulate and eloquent pacifist in the early Christian church."[2] Passages such as the following support such a claim:

The assertion that "certain Jews at the time of Christ revolted against the Jewish community and followed Jesus" is not less false than the claim "that the Jews had their origin in a revolt of certain Egyptians." Celsus and those who agree with him will not be able to cite a single act of rebellion on the part of the Christians. If a revolt had indeed given rise to the Christian community, if Christians took their origins from the Jews, who were allowed to take up arms in defense of their possessions and to kill their enemies, the Christian Lawgiver would not have made homicide absolutely forbidden. He would not have taught that his disciples were never justified in taking such action against a man even if he were the greatest wrongdoer. [Jesus] considered it contrary to his divinely inspired legislation to approve any kind of homicide whatsoever. If Christians had started with a revolt, they would never have submitted to the kind of peaceful laws which permitted them to be slaughtered "like sheep" (Psalm 44:11) and which made them always incapable of taking vengeance on their persecutors because they followed the law of gentleness and love. *(Against Celsus* 3.8)

To those who ask about our origin and our founder we reply that we have come in response to Jesus' commands to beat into plowshares the rational swords of conflict and arrogance and to change into pruning hooks those spears that we used to fight with. For we no longer take up the sword against any nation, nor do we learn the art of war any more. Instead of following the traditions that made us "strangers to the covenants" (Eph 2:12), we have become sons of peace through Jesus our founder. (*Against Celsus* 5.33)

Denying to the Jews of old, who had their own socio-political system and their own territory, the right to march against their enemies, to wage war in order to protect their traditions, to kill, or to impose some kind of punishment on adulterers, murderers and others who committed similar crimes would have been nothing short of consigning them to complete destruction when an enemy attacked their nation because their own Law would have sapped their strength and would have forestalled their resistance. But Providence, which in an earlier time gave us the Law and now has given us the Gospel of Jesus Christ, did not want the Jewish system perpetuated and so destroyed the city of the Jews and their temple along with the divine worship that was celebrated there through sacrifices and prescribed rites. *(Against Celsus 7.26)*

From these and from the longer passage we will quote shortly, we find for the first time a Christian writer wrestling with the practical sociopolitical as well as with the spiritual or theological ramifications of consistently following the NT call to nonviolence. It is all the more ironic, then, that it is in Origen that we can also find the roots of the medieval two-sword theory,[3] and that Origen himself also concedes some points that, in a changed context, were foundational for the later Christian just-war theory. Let us look more closely at the context of Origen's writing on this topic.

About A.D. 178, Celsus wrote his *The True Story (alēthēs logos),* the earliest known full-length anti-Christian polemic. A full six decades later, and at a time of relative peace for Christians in the empire, upon the urging of his patron, Ambrosius, Origen wrote a refutation. Origen's extensive quotations from the work of his otherwise-unrecorded adversary in the eight books *Against Celsus* allow us to reconstruct most of the structure and content of Celsus's attack. Celsus complained that the Christians were shirking their civic duties by refusing to take part in public or military life. Origen writes as if there had been no change in the situation from about A.D. 178 to 248. Like Tertullian, he argues that Christians by their prayers and good lives combat the devils and evil spirits which cause dissension and war, and that they thus fulfill their obligations to the empire.

In the next place, Celsus urges us "to help the king with all our might, and to labor with him in the maintenance of justice, to fight for him, and if he require it, to fight under him, or lead an army with him." To this our answer is, that we do, when occasion requires, give help to kings, and that, so to say, a divine help, "putting on the whole armor of God" (Eph 6:11). And this we do in obedience to the injunction of the apostle (Paul), "I exhort, therefore, that first of all, supplications, prayers, intercessions, and giving of thanks, be made for all men; for kings, and for all that are in authority" (1 Tim 2:1–2); and the more any one excells in piety, the more effective help does he render to kings, even more than is given by soldiers who go forth to fight and slay as many of the enemy as they can. And to those enemies of our faith who require us to bear arms for the commonwealth, and to slay men, we can reply: "Do not those who are priests at certain shrines, and those who attend on certain gods, as you account them, keep their hands free from blood, that they may with hands unstained and free from human blood offer the appointed sacrifices to your gods; and even when war is upon you, you never enlist the priests in the army. If that, then, is a laudable custom, how much more so, that while others are engaged in battle, these too should engage as the priests and ministers of God, keeping their hands pure, and wrestling in prayers to God on behalf of those who are fighting in a righteous cause, and for the king who reigns righteously, that whatever is opposed to those who act righteously may be destroyed!" And as we by our prayers vanquish all demons who stir up war, and lead us to the violation of oaths, and disturb the peace, we in this way are much more helpful to the kings than those who go into the field to fight for them. (*Against Celsus* 8.73)

This passage is representative of Origen's thought; it is in fact the best single passage through which to approach his attitudes toward war, peace, and military service. Of significance for the development toward what later came to be the dominant Christian just-war attitude is Origen's admission of the Christian's obligation to support "those who are fighting in a righteous cause." But because all Christians are "priests," it is not proper for them (no more than it is for pagan priests) to fight with anything but spiritual arms. Origen envisioned a world in which war and the need for force would disappear in proportion to the spread of Christianity. Thus the dilemma of Celsus (if all became Christian, no one would be left to protect the emperor) would never materialize. Living in an empire largely at peace, it was possible for a Christian to argue this way. Some wars could be conceived of as necessary, even "righteous," but basically as non-Christian or sub-Christian activities from which Christians must abstain.

But before going further, some remarks on Origen's hermeneutics are in order. While not denying that he is pervasively Platonic in the way he perceives reality and thinks, most contemporary Origen scholars agree that he is also, and indeed first and foremost, a biblical theologian. His central hermeneutical principle is Jesus Christ. By this Origen means primarily the *mystical* Christ, the Christ who has "passed over" to the Father and there continues to intercede for us and be with us in our transitus to the Father. This view is especially strong in his recently discovered and published *Passover Treatise (Peri Pascha)*.[4] There, consistent with what he has also insisted on elsewhere, the historical events of the past, the OT types, are seen as referring not to some already completed (or "dead") historical event of the past, but to the transitus or passing over of the Logos, the mystical Christ, to the Father and, connected with that, *our own* ongoing transitus.

In all this, of course, Origen had no knowledge that would enable him to understand the processes by which the Scriptures, especially in the OT, actually came to be. Unable to find a satisfactory literal meaning for the numerous wars and acts of violence in the OT, he spiritualizes them, most notably in his homilies on Joshua and Numbers,[5] by means of allegory. Since the spiritual meaning is always in reference to Christ, the OT wars and battles are seen as referring to the spiritual battle of Christ and the Christians against the evil powers and especially the demons who are the cause of sin and the things that lead to war.

This is the background of what Origen is saying and claiming in *Against Celsus* 8.70 and 73. Here Origen shares some important suppositions with his adversaries, the long-dead Celsus and the anti-Christian thinkers contemporaneous with Origen whom we must assume Origen also had in mind. These suppositions are: (1) a belief in the reality of the demons who are the internal and ultimate causes of war; (2) an in-principle admission of the need for civil order and the force needed to maintain it; (3) an admission that the wars of the emperor, particularly in the case of a good emperor, are just and necessary. The Christian's role in all this, however, is not to fight wars on behalf of the empire and the emperor, but to fight the much more important internal spiritual battle against the demons who cause the wars. Thus one can conclude that not only do Christians not abandon the emperor to his foes, they are actually fighting for him in the most important way possible. For if all were to become Christians, the need for force to defend the empire would, by that fact and to the extent of the conversion, have been eliminated.

One must begin an analysis of this position with the observation that *Origen accepts the fact of Celsus's complaint* that Christians do not serve in the army. Origen defends Christianity not by denying the charge but by defending the rightness of the Christian position. The evidence that at least some Christians served in the military was quite strong by the time Origen wrote. He himself had traveled widely and was not without contact with official Roman circles. It is hard to imagine him being unaware of Christians in the military. He was something of a rigorist, however, although not in the legalistic way that Tertullian was. He may have chosen to defend, for the purposes of his polemic, only what he perceived to be the ideal Christian stance rather than what he knew to be the actual situation.

Be that as it may, one can only say that his theory of an increasing Christianization carrying with it a decreasing need for military force is indeed a beautiful and hopeful conception. But alas, it did not work out that way. One might indeed observe, since the world as a whole has never become truly Christian, that the theory has never been proven false. But that is speculation in the wind. Whatever merit the theory might have had in Origen's day, the critical hindsight available to us suggests that the theory, in terms of any practical value, was flawed from the outset. From the understanding that modern Christians have of human nature, society, and the world, from our experience of the way salvation is worked out in this world, we can only conclude that Origen's vision, for all its beauty, was unrealistic. It never could have come about.

This being the case, what are the consequences of Origen's position for the subsequent development of Christian thought and for our situation today? *First*, one of the most fundamental premises of the just-war theory, namely that there is or can be a just and righteous cause that can be defended by arms, is conceded from the outset. *Second*, he viewed war and the use of military force as a pre-Christian (OT/Jewish) or sub-Christian (pagan/Roman) reality. What was necessary or allowable in the OT is now no longer so since the coming of Christ. And what is still necessary and allowable for order and peace in a world not yet Christian, is not allowable (nor, in Origen's vision, needed) for those who have already accepted Christ. *Third*, Origen readily admits the responsibility of the Christian to help carry the burdens of establishing and maintaining order and peace. *Fourth*, he locates this responsibility entirely in the internal and spiritual realm of being. He becomes a major mediator to the Christian tradition of the idea of spiritual warfare found in Ephesians 6. *Fifth*, he becomes a particularly powerful mediator to the later tradition of the concept of the specifically or ideally Christian vocation and activity as something internal, spiritual, distinct, and separate from worldly pursuits, as opposed to public, practical, and secular pursuits. These views did not, of course, originate with Origen, but he in fact contributed massively to the otherworldly flavor of Christian monastic and ascetic ideals. Thus, when Origen's vision of a Christian world in which war had become obsolete did not materialize, many of the assumptions and concessions he had made in his own historical context inexorably drove later Christian thinkers away from pacifist and toward just-war positions.

In all this, two fundamental sets of tensions were left unresolved to work their often infelicitous effects on later Christian doctrine and life. On the practical side was the tension between Christianity's practical ideals of perfection and the demands and needs of life in the world. When this tension was resolved by practical compromise, the full pursuit of Christian perfection was relegated to those who left the world for the religious or monastic state of perfection. Where compromise was refused, the result was too often a marginalized sectarianism. On the theoretical side, the tension was between Jewish-Christian creational and Christian incarnational faith on the one hand, and a fundamentally antimaterial, antiworldly Platonic way of thinking on the other. Simplistically put, the faith of Origen and most of the fathers was creational and incarnational, a faith which called them to see God present and working in this material world, and to eschew radical dichotomies between matter and spirit. But their thinking and understanding were primarily in Platonic modes that saw the material world and all associated with it either as a lower form of reality or even inherently evil or sinful. Neither in Origen nor later have these tensions been fundamentally resolved. A certain amount of theoretical or doctrinal resolution of these has been achieved (witness Vatican II's Pastoral Constitution on the Church in the Modern World), but it is obvious that no theoretical Christian consensus on these tensions has yet been achieved, let alone agreement on practical strategies.

NOTES

1. The best brief introduction to Origen is H. Crouzel, "Origen and Origenism," in *New Catholic Encyclopedia* (New York: McGraw-Hill, 1967) 10:767–74. At greater length, Joseph Wilson Trigg, *Origen: The Bible and Philosophy in the Third-Century Church* (Atlanta: John Knox Press, 1983). For an introduction to Origen's writings themselves, H. Urs von Balthasar, *Origen. Spirit and Fire: An Anthology of His Writings*, trans. R. Daly (Washington, D.C.: Catholic University of America Press, 1984).

2. Louis J. Swift, *The Early Fathers on War and Military Service*, Message of the Fathers of the Church 19 (Wilmington, Del.: Michael Glazier, 1983), 60.

3. Cf. G. E. Caspary, *Politics and Exegesis: Origen and the Two Swords* (Berkeley, Los Angeles, and London: University of California Press, 1979).

4. O. Guéraud and P. Nautin, eds., *Origène sur la Pâque. Traité inédit publié d'après un papyrus de Toura*, Christianisme antique 2 (Paris: Gabriel Beauchesne, 1979).

5. A. von Harnack's *Militia Christi: The Christian Religion and the Military in the First Three Centuries*, trans. D. Mc L. Gracie (Philadelphia: Fortress Press, 1981), 47–52, provides a reliable summary of Origen's teaching on this point (see also above, chap. 2 on military metaphors).

7.

The Apocryphal Gospels

Pacifist scholars have often made the comment that it would be difficult to see Christian soldiers enlisting in the army because they were aware of Jesus' teachings about nonviolence and love. This consideration especially explains why there is so little evidence for Christians in the military during the first two centuries. It would be "assumed" that one simply would not enlist.

In response, it must be said that the relative lack of evidence might just as easily be explained by the relative lack of Christians at that time. But as to the assumption that early Christians possessed uncommon moral virtues that have been lost through the centuries, this expresses a romantic view that is neither justified nor possible to prove. The early church in modern research is coming to appear increasingly pluralistic. One example of this diversity of perspectives is to be found in the apocryphal gospels. This material is of importance to our investigation in that it differs strikingly from the common opinion that the early Christians were totally pacifistic. The picture of Jesus in this literature, if one might call it that, moves in an almost totally opposite direction from that of the canonical gospels. Moreover, the stories of Jesus in the apocryphal gospels were apparently the products of a lively oral tradition; many of them are repeated from document to document. Until the direction of early church scholarship shifted to the point where sociology and psychology gained a respectable following, the study of these documents was bypassed by historians of doctrine who treated them only in footnotes suggesting that the theology contained therein was crude and vulgar. Until the social sciences recorded their votes, there was little to prevent the history of doctrine from reproducing an overly romanticized picture of this segment of church history.

The Jesus of this literature, then, was a strikingly violent figure.

Revenge and the ostentatious application of power animates him.
Rather than turning the other cheek, Jesus seems to turn the cheeks of
the others who offend him, frequently for slight insults. Although it is
difficult to prove, one gets the impression that these stories come from
a powerless illiterate crowd which fanaticized retribution. Were they
to gain power, violence would likely be the result. This kind of person
finds a special attraction to the military way of dealing with conflict. To
fill out the picture, there are power motifs in the apocryphals which
are not violent but take excitement in power over the inanimate, such
as clay sparrows made to fly and broken things magically fixed. In a
word, this literature communicates the theme of mechanical power to
neutralize frustration. The following excerpts from the *Infancy Gospel
of Thomas* illustrate this graphically. The same stories are repeated, for
example, in Pseudo-Matthew (28–29).

THE ACCOUNT OF THOMAS THE ISRAELITE PHILOSOPHER CONCERNING THE CHILDHOOD OF THE LORD[1]

1. I, Thomas the Israelite, tell and make known to you all, brethren from
among the Gentiles, all the works of the childhood of our Lord Jesus Christ
and his mighty deeds, which he did when he was born in our land. The
beginning is as follows.

2.1 When this boy Jesus was five years old he was playing at the ford of a
brook, and he gathered together into pools the water that flowed by, and made
it at once clean, and commanded it by his word alone. 2. He made soft clay
and fashioned from it twelve sparrows. And it was the sabbath when he did
this. And there were also many other children playing with him. 3. Now when
a certain Jew saw what Jesus was doing in his play on the sabbath, he at once
went and told his father Joseph: "See, your child is at the brook, and he has
taken clay and fashioned twelve birds and has profaned the sabbath." 4. And
when Joseph came to the place and saw (it), he cried out to him saying: "Why
do you do on the sabbath what ought not to be done?" But Jesus clapped his
hands and cried to the sparrows: "Off with you!" And the sparrows took flight
and went away chirping. 5. The Jews were amazed when they saw this, and
went away and told their elders what they had seen Jesus do.

3.1 But the son of Annas the scribe was standing there with Joseph; and he
took a branch of a willow and (with it) dispersed the water which Jesus had
gathered together. 2. When Jesus saw what he had done he was enraged and
said to him: "You insolent, godless dunderhead, what harm did the pools and
the water do to you? See, now you also shall wither like a tree and shall bear
neither leaves nor root nor fruit." 3. And immediately that lad withered up
completely; and Jesus departed and went into Joseph's house. But the parents
of him that was withered took him away, bewailing his youth, and brought him
to Joseph and reproached him: "What a child you have, who does such things."

4.1 After this again he went through the village, and a lad ran and knocked
against his shoulder. Jesus was exasperated and said to him: "You shall not go
further on your way," and the child immediately fell down and died. But some,

who saw what took place, said: "From where does this child spring, since his every word is an accomplished deed?" 2. And the parents of the dead child came to Joseph and blamed him and said: "Since you have such a child, you cannot dwell with us in the village; or else teach him to bless and not to curse. For he is slaying our children."

14.1 And when Joseph saw the understanding of the child and his age, that he was growing to maturity, he resolved again that he should not remain ignorant of letters; and he took him and handed him over to another teacher. And the teacher said to Joseph: "First I will teach him Greek, and then Hebrew." For the teacher knew the child's knowledge and was afraid of him. Nevertheless he wrote the alphabet and practised it with him for a long time; but he gave him no answer. 2. And Jesus said to him: "If you are indeed a teacher, and if you know the letters well, tell me the meaning of the Alpha, and I will tell you that of the Beta." And the teacher was annoyed and struck him on the head. And the child was hurt and cursed him, and he immediately fainted and fell to the ground on his face. 3. And the child returned to Joseph's house. But Joseph was grieved and commanded his mother: "Do not let him go outside the door, for all those who provoke him die."

This does not mean that the apocryphal gospels are now to be considered as the key sources for studying popular religious psychology among early Christians. But they can no longer be discounted as insignificant, and they may indeed have been far more expressive of the popular religious psychology of the time than, say, the television soaps are of the popular psychology of the American people.

NOTES

1. Edgar Hennecke, *New Testament Apocrypha*, ed. William Schnee-melcher; Eng. trans. and ed. R. McL. Wilson (Philadelphia: Westminster Press, 1963) 1:392–93, 397.

8.

Roman Army Religion

The reason that many church historians have given little attention to idolatry as the basic conflict between the church and the Roman military is because they knew little or nothing about the nature and extent of Roman army religion. To people accustomed to separating church and state, such a consideration does not come naturally. Not only do they miss the fact that modern military systems are bound together by a glue of ritual and tradition, but they also tend to pass off the Roman rituals as superstition not worthy of the time to learn how they work. This is unfortunate since the story of the relationship between the church and the Roman army cannot properly be told without understanding this dynamic.

As was the case with other significant aspects of Roman life, the army had a religious structure that informed nearly everything it did.[1] This religious structure had several chief functions. First, it created a sacred cosmos in which the soldier lived from the day he entered until he died; even veterans participated in this world. It separated the soldier from the civilian, Roman territory from enemy, and cosmos from chaos. The walls around the camp formed the boundary that enclosed this sacred world; entering a camp over the walls and not through the gate was punishable by death. Second, it provided models of what it meant to be a good soldier and how to show respect to the gods and the emperor, their representative. Third, it furnished a host of abstract deities—*Honos, Virtus, Pietas,* and *Disciplina.* These abstract deities are regularly found in dedicatory inscriptions. Fourth, army religion helped in the Roman army, as in any other army, to control the natural fear of death in the soldiers' lives. Ritual behavior, of course, is a great distraction as well as a means of dissipating guilt. The Roman soldier no doubt shined brass as have soldiers of all time. Rituals in setting up the camp not only had the value of helping soldiers know their position in camp but created a sense of order to allay anxiety. So the world of the soldier had a system in which strategic, tactical, and ritual considerations dovetailed so completely that any attempt to separate them would be futile.

In describing the various features of this religious world, historians have traditionally used the classifications of official and unofficial army religion. The official religious observances were kept uniform throughout the empire. One reason for this was that centurions were continuously being transferred from legion to legion, so the similarity from place to place made them feel at home and secure. Then too, the army brought in soldiers from a plethora of cultural backgrounds; the religion of the army "Romanized" these people. Unofficial army religion refers to the cults and observances that the soldiers brought along with them. It was army policy that these be kept outside the walls of the camp.[2] No doubt these combined with the prostitutes, pimps, gamblers, and con men who followed every legion around to produce the moral cacophony that Tertullian so abhorred. Of the unofficial observances perhaps that of Mithra is the most famous, as the comments of Tertullian indicate.

To turn to the components of official army religion, the one that first strikes the eye is the cult of the standards. Of these, the chief standard was the eagle (*aquila*) symbolizing Jupiter Optimus Maximus who protected the entire empire. Anywhere the eagle is an auspicious creature and it certainly was that for the army. This standard was the one on which the esprit de corps of the legion rested. To lose the eagle in a battle meant that the legion responsible would be disbanded in disgrace if there was anything left of it at battle's end. Once lost, the Romans did not forget it until the standard was returned; it was thirty-two years in the case of the one lost in Germany in A.D. 9.[3] The eagle and other lesser standards of the centuries were the object of a cult, the *Rosalae Signarum*—the days in May when the troops garlanded them. We possess numerous inscriptions that are dedicated to the genius of the standards.

To the Deities of the Emperors and the Genius of the Second Legion August, in honor of the eagle, the senior Centurion gave this gift. (*C.I.L.* VII, 103)

To the Genius and the standards of the First Loyal Cohort of Vardulli, Roman Citizens, part-mounted, one thousand strong, Titus Licinius Valerianus, Tribune. (*C.I.L.* VII, 1031)

In the following inscription, the birthday of the legion is symbolized by the reference to the birthday of the eagle.

To Juppiter Optimus Maximus, a vexillation of the legion VII Gemina Felix under the direction of Junius Victor a centurion of this same legion for the birthday of the eagle. (*C.I.L.* II, 6183)

These inscriptions are examples of how soldiers gave thanks for victories won. The gods would then respond with favors as well as with continued success for the legions. Often a soldier would vow to the gods that, if he got out of a tight scrape, he would dedicate an inscription to them. This so-called bargain model was quite common in Roman religious practice: sacrifices were offered to the gods who then returned favors.

The cult of the standards did not escape the attention of Tertullian who made the following statements about it.

The camp religion of the Romans is all through a worship of the standards, a setting the standards above all gods. (Tertullian *Apology* 16.8)

... it [the religion of the camp] adores the standards, they swear by the standards, they prefer them to Juppiter himself. (Tertullian *Ad nationes* 12)

The *sacramentum* was the military oath recited upon enlistment and twice a year thereafter for the remainder of a soldier's time of service. In republican times *sacramentum* meant an oath or a bonded agreement between two parties. The agreement eventually came to be considered sacred. The history of the word then gives us a suggestion about how the same word can apply to both the military oath of allegiance and the rites of baptism and eucharist. In the army one who broke the oath was regarded as *nefas,* liable to punishment from men and the gods; such a person was beyond the protection of the law and legally a fair target for anyone who wished practice.

Before the imperial period, soldiers took the oath to individual generals. On account of problems of potential insurrection and the generals using the troops for their personal ambitions, the oath later was given only to the emperor. Since the emperors were also appointed to the office of *Pontifex Maximus,* the *sacramentum* involved implicit idolatry in Christian minds. The oath demanded unquestioned obedience to the emperor as the highest authority. Tertullian expressed it this way:

There is no agreement between the divine and human sacrament, between the standard of Christ and the standard of the devil, between the camp of light and the camp of darkness. (*On Idolatry* 19.2)

In addition, it would appear that the oath was taken in the context of an entire military system, because there exists evidence that the soldiers occasionally took an oath to the standards of the legion as well.[4] Such an oath does not contradict what has been said about the oath given to the emperor. By virtue of his title of *imperator* the emperor was the final authority, the commander in chief of everything that happened in that military system. From a Christian viewpoint, however, there would not be much difference between taking an oath to the emperor or the standards—both would appear idolatrous.

We learned a great deal about the liturgical nature of army religion with the discovery of the *Feriale Duranum*—a calendar of army religious festivals for the year A.D. 226.[5] Although only about half of the year was intact, it is possible to conjecture the rest of it. Specified in it were the festivals and the nature of the sacrifice to be done at each. The existence of the calendar leads us to the conclusion that a similar document went out annually to each legion or, at least, to each cohort of the ⌐ ¬ny. The intended effect was to synchronize the worship of the various units with that of Rome, a practice already assumed by the church in its battle over the date of Easter.[6] Although irregularly spaced, the frequency of religious festivals averaged about one every ten days.

The following is a translation of the *Feriale Duranum*. If we had no other evidence relating to Roman army religion, this document would be sufficient to prove that the Christian in the army was caught in a religious net of exceedingly fine mesh. Listed in it are various observances relating to the imperial cult and army religion. Some of the festivals originated far back in republican times, such as the Rose-festival (May 9 and 31, honoring the dead) or the taking of the oath (January 3). The antiquity of some of these festivals indicates that the Roman army, like most armies, placed great emphasis on tradition; armies are frequently conservative. Whether consciously intended or not, the calendar of festivals had the effect of Romanizing the army. If this was consciously done there should be no surprise: the armies took soldiers from all parts of the expanding empire. These recruits, Christians included, had to be made to look at things from a Roman perspective.[7]

FERIALE DURANUM[8]

Col. i

1   January 1—
2–6   January 3. Because vows are paid and undertaken both for the welfare of our Lord Marcus Aurelius Severus Alexander Augustus and for the

eternity of the empire of the Roman nation, [to Jupiter Optimus Maximus an ox, to Juno Regina a cow, to Minerva a cow, to Jupiter Victor] an ox [to Juno Sospes? a cow, – – – to Mars Pater a bull, to Mars Victor] a bull, to Victoria a cow [

7–9   January 7. [Because honorable discharge with the enjoyment of (customary)] privileges [is given to men who have served their time] or (because) stipendia are counted [for the soldiers, to Jupiter Optimus Maximus an ox, to Juno a cow, to Minerva] a cow, to Salus a cow, to Mars Pater a bull [

10   January 8. For the birthday of the deified (empress) [to the deified (empress) [   ] a supplicatio.

11–12 January [9–23]. For the birthday of Lucius [. . . .] Caesar, [   ] of Lucius [. . . .] Caesar.

13   January 24. For the birthday [of the deified Hadrian, to the deified Hadrian an ox.]

14–16 January 28. For the [– – – and] very great Parthian victory of the deified Severus and for [the accession of the deified Trajan, to Victoria] Parthica a cow, to the deified Trajan [an ox].

17–18 February 4. For the accession [of the deified Antonius Magnus] a supplicatio; to the deified Antoninus an ox.

19–20 March 1. For the [birthday] ceremonies [of Mars Pater Victor to Mars] Pater Victor a bull.

21–22 March 7. For the accession [of the deified Marcus Antoninus and the deified Lucius Verus], to the deified Marcus an ox, [to the deified Lucius] an ox.

23–26 March 13. [Because] the Emperor [Caesar Marcus Aurelius Severus Alexander] was named emperor, to Jupiter an ox, [to Juno a cow, to Minerva a cow – – –] to Mars an ox; [because] Alexander our Augustus was saluted as Imperator [for the first time] by the soldiers [of the Emperor Augustus Marcus Aurelius Severus Alexander, a supplicato – – –].

27–28 [March 14.] Because Alexander our [Augustus] was named [Augustus and Pater Patriae and] Pontifex Maximus, a supplicatio; [to the Genius of our Lord] Alexander [Augustus a bull – – –].

Col. ii

1   March 19. For the day of the Quinquatria, a supplicatio; until March 23, supplicationes.

2   April 4. For the birthday of the deified Antoninus Magnus, to the deified Antoninus an ox.

3   April 9. For the accession of the deified Pius Severus, to the deified Pius Severus an ox.

4   April 11. For the birthday of the deified Pius Severus, to the deified [Pius] Severus an ox.

5   April 21. For the birthday of the Eternal City of Rome, [to the Eternal City of Rome a cow].

6   April 26. For the birthday of the deified Marcus Antoninus, to [the deified Marcus] Antoninus [an ox].

7   May 7. For the birthday of the deified Julia Maesa, to [the deified] Maesa [a supplicatio].

8   May [9–11]. For the Rose-festival of the standards, a supplicatio.

9   May 12. For the circus-races in honor of Mars, to Mars Pater Ultor a bull.

10–11 May 21. Because the deified Severus was saluted as Imperator by [. . . . , – – –] to the deified Pius Severus.

12–13 May 24. For the birthday of Germanicus Caesar, a supplicatio to the memory of Germanicus Caesar.

14   May 31. For the Rose-festival of the standards, a supplicatio.

15   June [9]. For the Vestalia, to Vesta Mater a supplicatio.

16–17 June [26]. Because our Lord Marcus Aurelius Severus Alexander was named Caesar and clothed in the toga virilis, to the Genius of Alexander Augustus a bull.

18   July [1]. Because Alexander our Augustus was designated consul for the first time, a supplicatio.

19   July [2–5]. For the birthday of the deified Matidia, to the deified Matidia a supplicatio.

20   July [10]. For the accession of the deified Antoninus Pius, to the deified Antoninus an ox.

21   July [12]. For the birthday of the deified Julius, to the deified Julius an ox.

22   July [23]. For the day of the Neptunalia, a supplicatio (and) a sacrifice.

23–24 [August 1. For] the birthday of the deified Claudius and the deified Pertinax, to the deified Claudius an ox; [to the deified Pertinax] an ox.

25   [August 5.] For [the circus-races] in honor of Salus, to Salus [a cow].

26   August [14–29. For] the birthday of Mammea [Augusta] mother of our Augustus, to the Juno of Mammea Augusta [a cow].

27   *No coherent text.*

28   August [15–30]. For the birthday of the deified Marciana, [to the deified] Marciana [a supplicatio].

Col. iii

1   [August] 31. [For] the birthday [of the deified Commodus, to the deified] Commodus [an ox].

2   September [7?].

4–5 September [18]. For [the birthday of the deified Trajan and the accession of the deified Nerva, to the deified Trajan an ox, to the deified Nerva an ox].

6   [September 19.] For [the birthday of the deified] Antoninus [Pius, to the deified Antoninus an ox].

7   September [20–22]. For the birthday of the deified Faustina, to the deified Faustina a supplicatio.

8   September [23]. For the birthday of the deified [Augustus], to the deified Augustus [an ox].

12   October 16–November 12.

Col. iv

7   December [16] – – – birthday? – – – supplicatio
8   until December 23.

As we have already mentioned, the camp was a Roman religious world, a microcosm of Rome itself. Accordingly, the ritual castrametation required everything in the camp to be placed in relationship to the *praetorium* and the main gate. The *praetorium* was a symbolic double of the Capitoline hill in Rome; it also housed the *aedes*, which was the sacred repository of the standards and images of the emperor. Located in the center of the camp, the *praetorium* was the dwelling of the commander of the legion. From there every parade formed. On the march, even for overnight, the same relationships and proportions were staked out so the camp would be a portable sacred city. The walls were either ditched or constructed from the soldiers' baggage. A permanent camp, of course, would have ditches and impregnable stone walls. Since army policy forbade unofficial cults inside the walls, it would have been most difficult for a Christian to practice his religion inside the camp unless, of course, he could keep everything in his head. Tertullian saw all this and expressed it in his opposition of the camp of light to the camp of darkness.

Ceremonies and festivals could be dangerous times for the Christian, particularly because of the meticulous uniformity required of the soldiers. Of course, this was where the soldier not wearing the crown got caught (see our treatment of Tertullian's *Treatise on the Crown* in chap. 3 above). Most likely, the festival brought to a head what had simmered inside him for some time. The uniform was a powerful symbol and each part of the uniform—belt, sword, the centurion's vine switch—had special associations. When Marcellus threw off these three, the official account of his trial said that by doing this he had violated his *sacramentum* (see below in chap. 9). That is how strict and interlaced the army was about matters of discipline. Discipline, literally, was worshiped, which was probably what led Vegetius to say that the Roman soldiers were not the largest or strongest, but they were the most disciplined, so they won more battles.

The totality of Roman army religion was an impressive system, one so thoroughly comprehensive that it would be impossible for any Christian in the army to avoid dealing with it in one way or another. The church fathers who objected to army religion may have dissuaded some Christians from entering the army to seek its benefits—citizenship, retirement stipend, and a plot of farm land. Others enlisted but found things binding on their consciences and objected. These were the people we call military martyrs; none left the service alive without being discharged at the end of their enlistment period—twenty years in the legions, twenty-five in the auxiliary forces. And then there were those whom we know to have been Christian and stayed in for the full length of service. How they did it we can only conjecture. Probably they modeled their Christianity along the lines of Roman polytheism— Mars is for victory, spring nymphs are for fresh water, Jupiter Dolichenus is for weapons that do not break in combat, and Christ is for when your weapon does break and you die. Not theologically sophisticated, to be sure; but as is the case with the apocryphal gospels, it does point out the pitfalls of trying to tell the whole story solely from the perspective of the fathers.

NOTES

1. For the thorough statement, see J. Helgeland, "Roman Army Religion," *ANRW* 2.16.2, pp. 1470–1505.

2. A. S. Hoey, "Official Policy towards Oriental Cults in the Roman Army," *Transactions and Proceedings of the American Philological Association* 70 (1939): 458–81, here 463–64.

3. G. Webster, *The Roman Imperial Army* (London: A. & C. Black, 1969), 135.

4. C. E. Brand, *Roman Military Law* (Austin: University of Texas Press, 1968), 92.

5. Robert O. Fink, *Roman Military Records on Papyrus*, The American Philological Association Monograph 26 (Cleveland: Press of Case Western Reserve University, 1971), 422–29.

6. See J. Helgeland, "Time and Space: Christian and Roman," *ANRW* 2.23.2, pp. 1285–1305, here 1299–1300.

7. A. D. Nock, "The Roman Army and the Roman Religious Year," *Harvard Theological Review* 45 (1952): 187–252.

8. The translation is from Fink, *Roman Military Records,* 428–29 (see n. 5 above).

9.

The Military Martyrs

We possess a number of authentic accounts of Christian soldiers who were martyred. Statistically they fall for the most part in the reign of the emperor Diocletian (284–305) and many come from the church in North Africa. Toward the end of the third century there was an increasing pressure from both the Roman and Christian sides that occasioned this cluster of martyrdoms. The empire, increasingly troubled by a series of political, economic, and military setbacks during that century, felt the need for conservative policies, particularly in religious matters. Decius (249–51) and Diocletian both tried to create a uniformity in religion that, they hoped, would bring divine favor on the empire and reverse its downhill course. The pressure from the Christian side owed to their rapidly increasing population and expanding ecclesiastical network. The forty years before the Great Persecution had been a time of relative tranquility for the church; in 260 Gallienus discontinued the policy of bloody persecution and switched rather to attempting to ridicule the church into submission. While the policy he began and his successors maintained continued to fail, the church continued to grow. A confrontation seemed inevitable.

It came to a head with Diocletian. We have no evidence to prove directly that he was the one who first began to tighten the policies on religious discipline in the army, for there were, in fact, martyrdoms of soldiers before the time of Diocletian and eight years before the Great Persecution. At the very least we can say that with Diocletian religion came more and more to center stage. The first incident, however, the martyrdom of Marinus, occurred some years earlier.

Eusebius tells of a soldier, Marinus, about to be promoted to centurion (*Ecclesiastical History* 7.15). If Eusebius has placed this account in the correct chronological order in his narrative, the year was approximately 260. Marinus was about to accept his promotion to the rank of centurion but was accused of being a Christian and, as such, could not be counted upon to lead the sacrifices expected of centurions. There are several striking features of this account. If Marinus had not been stopped, he most likely would have accepted his promotion without difficulty and we would not even know his name today. We may also infer that the soldier who accused Marinus had some experience with Christians; possibly Christians in the service had been caught in this bind before. Since Marinus was about to be promoted to centurion we can say that he had been in the army for some time, but how long as a Christian we cannot tell. Centurions were always seasoned soldiers.

THE MARTYRDOM OF ST. MARINUS[1]

During their time [i.e., of Pope Xystus, ca. 260] the churches everywhere enjoyed peace. Yet at Caesarea in Palestine, a man named Marinus, who had been honoured with many posts in the army and was known for his wealth and his good family, was beheaded for his witness to Christ. It came about in the following way. Among the Romans the vine branch is a mark of honour; and those that obtain it, they believe, become centurions. An army post fell vacant, and according to the order of promotion it was Marinus who was entitled to fill it. But when he was on the point of receiving the office, another man came up before the magistrate and attacked Marinus, saying that as a Christian Marinus would not sacrifice to the emperors, and should therefore not be allowed to share in honours that belonged to the Romans according to the ancient laws; but that instead the post should fall to himself.

It is said that the magistrate (whose name was Achaeus) was moved by this, and he first asked Marinus what views he held. And then, when he saw that he persistently confessed that he was a Christian, he granted him a stay of three hours to reconsider. No sooner had Marinus left the court than Theotecnus, the bishop of Caesarea, approached and drew him aside in conversation; taking him by the hand he led him to the church. Once inside, he placed Marinus right in front of the altar, and drawing aside Marinus' cloak pointed to the sword attached to his side. At the same time he brought a copy of the divine Gospels and he set it before Marinus, asking him to choose which he preferred. Without hesitation Marinus put out his right hand and took the divine writings.

"So then," said Theotecnus, "hold fast, hold fast to God, and given strength by him, may you obtain what you have chosen. Now go in peace." [Cf. Acts 16:36]

No sooner had Marinus returned than a herald cried out to summon him before the tribunal; for the allotted time was now over. Marinus presented himself before the judge and showed even greater loyalty to the faith; and immediately, just as he was, he was led off to execution, and so found his fulfillment.

The next account, the *Acts of Maximilian,* refers to an event in the province of Mauretania on 12 March 295. The father of Maximilian brought him forward to be inducted, but the youth balked at the proceedings on account of the religious symbolism involved in the army, in particular the lead seal, which probably had the bust of the emperor struck on it.[2] It is interesting to note that the proconsul Dion knew about other Christians in the imperial bodyguard who had no problem in serving.

This account is regarded as being reliable because it fits the form of *acta* which were the minutes of a trial taken down by a court scribe. The first few sentences tell the place, date, and persons involved in the trial. The last three paragraphs are additions by Christians who wanted to connect the grave of Maximilian to the cult of saints' relics. Such graves were regarded as places where grace was concentrated, and thus were sought out for purposes of healing.

THE ACTS OF MAXIMILIAN[3]

1. On the twelfth day of March at Tebessa, in the consulship of Tuscus and Anullinus, Fabius Victor was summoned to the forum together with Maximilian; Pompeianus was permitted to act as their advocate.

The advocate spoke: "Fabius Victor, agent in charge of the recruiting tax, is present for his hearing along with Valerian Quintianus, imperial representative, and Victor's son Maximilian, an excellent recruit. Seeing that Maximilian has good recommendations, I request that he be measured."

The Proconsul Dion said: "What is your name?"

Maximilian replied: "But why do you wish to know my name? I cannot serve because I am a Christian."

The Proconsul Dion said: "Get him ready."

While he was being made ready, Maximilian replied: "I cannot serve. I cannot commit a sin. I am a Christian."

"Let him be measured," said the Proconsul Dion.

After he was measured, one of the staff said: "He is five foot ten."

Dion said to his staff: "Let him be given the military seal."

Still resisting, Maximilian replied: "I will not do it! I cannot serve!"

2. "Serve, or you will die," said Dion.

"I shall not serve," said Maximilian. "You may cut off my head, I will not serve this world, but only my God."

The Proconsul Dion, said: "Who has turned your head?"

"My own soul," said Maximilian, "and the one who has called me."

Dion said to Victor, the boy's father: "Speak to your son."

Victor said: "He is aware and can take his own counsel on what is best for him" (cf. John 9:23).

Dion said to Maximilian: "Agree to serve and receive the military seal."

"I will not accept the seal," he replied. "I already have the seal of Christ who is my God."

Dion said: "I shall send you to your Christ directly."

"I only wish you would," he replied. "This would be my glory."

Dion addressed his staff: "Let him be given the seal."

Maximilian resisted and said: "I will not accept the seal of this world; and, if you give it to me, I shall break it, for it is worthless, I am a Christian, I cannot wear a piece of lead around my neck after I have received the saving sign of Jesus Christ my Lord, the son of the living God. You do not know him; yet he suffered for our salvation; God delivered him up for our sins (cf. Acts 2:22–4; Rom 8:32). He is the one whom all we Christians serve: we follow him as the prince of life and the author of salvation."

"You must serve," said Dion, "and accept the seal—otherwise you will die miserably."

"I shall not perish," said Maximilian. "My name is already before my Lord. I may not serve."

Dion said: "Have regard for your youth: serve. This is what a young man should do."

"My service is for my Lord," Maximilian replied. "I cannot serve the world (cf. Matt 6:24, Luke 16:13). I have already told you: I am a Christian."

The Proconsul Dion said: "In the sacred bodyguard of our lords Diocletian and Maximian, Constantius and Maximus, there are soldiers who are Christian, and they serve."

Maximilian replied: "They know what is best for them. But I am a Christian and I cannot do wrong."

"What wrong do they commit," said Dion, "who serve in the army?"

Maximilian replied: "Why, you know what they do."

The Proconsul Dion said: "Serve. If you despise the military service you will perish miserably."

Maximilian replied: "I shall not perish, and if I depart from this world, my soul lives with Christ my Lord."

3. "Strike out his name!" said Dion. And when his name had been struck out, Dion said: "Because you have refused military service out of disloyalty, you will receive a suitable sentence as an example to the others." Then he read the following decision from a tablet: "Whereas Maximilian has disloyally refused the military oath, he is sentenced to die by the sword."

"Thank God!" said Maximilian.

He had lived in this world twenty-one years, three months, and eighteen days. And when he was led to the spot, he said: "My dearest brothers, hasten with all eagerness, with as much courage as you can, that it may be given to you to see the Lord, and that he may reward you with a similar crown."

Then with a joyous countenance he turned and said to his father: "Give this executioner my new clothes which you prepared for my military service. Then I shall receive you with my division of a hundred (cf. Matt 19:29) and we shall glory with the Lord together."

Soon afterwards he died. A woman named Pompeiana obtained his body from the magistrate and, after placing it in her own chamber, later brought it to Carthage. There she buried it at the foot of a hill near the governor's palace next to the body of the martyr Cyprian. Thirteen days later the woman herself passed away and was buried in the same spot. But Victor, the boy's father, returned to his home in great joy, giving thanks to God (cf. 1 Matt 4:24) that he had sent ahead a gift to the Lord, since he himself was soon to follow.

Thanks be to God! Amen.

For *The Acts of Marcellus* the manuscript tradition is a tangle, although of the two recensions—M and N—N is the one that makes most sense when compared with standard army procedures.[4] For our purposes, however, both recensions agree on the essentials. The year was 298. Arrested in Spain, Marcellus was transferred to Tingis in Mauretania Tingitana, across from the Rock of Gibraltar. At a festival dedicated to the birthdays of the emperors Diocletian and Maximian, Marcellus broke his vine switch and said that he could not do service (*militarem*) under any other oath than the one he had taken to Christ. The vine switch was the symbol of the centurion's authority. There was a parade that involved the standards of the legion; we have already seen how the standards fit Tertullian's conception of idolatry. Since the whole of the uniform was expected to be worn for festivals it had religious significance; throwing down his belt along with the sword was a symbolic act because the belt (*cingulum*) was the symbol of the military life. Of course, the phrase "the sacred ears of Diocletian and Maximian" needs no explanation. What made Marcellus's protest especially vivid was that he was a centurion in the first cohort indicating that he had been centurion long enough and had a clean record in order to be promoted that high. The specifications of the court underscore his high rank since he had "defiled the oath of the centurion's rank in which he served."

THE ACTS OF MARCELLUS (RECENSION N)[5]

The passion of St. Marcellus the martyr, who suffered at Leon in the Province of Gallecia under the governor Fortunatus on 30 October.

1. Just before the first day of August, in the consulship of Faustus and Gallus in the camp of the *legio VII Gemina,* Marcellus of the city of Hasta Regia was brought in, and Fortunatus said: "Why did you decide to take off your belt and throw it down with your sword and your staff?"

2. "I have already told you," Marcellus replied. "Before the standards of this legion when you were celebrating the holiday of your empire I answered publicly and in a loud voice confessed that I was a Christian, and that I could not fight by any other oath, but solely for the Lord Christ Jesus, Son of God almighty."

"I cannot conceal your rash act," said Fortunatus, "and hence I shall report this to the sacred ears of our lords Diocletian and Maximian, the most invincible Augusti, and to the most noble Caesars, Constantine and Licinius. But you shall be handed over to the court of the praetorian prefect, the lord Aurelius Agricolanus, under the guard of the soldier Caecilius Arva."

3. On 30 October in the consulship of Faustus and Gallus at Tingis, when Marcellus of the city of Hasta Regia was brought in, one of the court secretaries announced: "Here before the court is Marcellus, whom the governor Fortunatus has handed over to your jurisdiction. He is submitted to your

Excellency. There is also a letter here from Fortunatus, which I shall read with your permission."

Agricolanus said: "Read it."

The court clerk said: "It has already been read."

4. Agricolanus said: "Did you say the things reported in the governor's official proceedings?"

"I did," replied Marcellus.

Agricolanus said: "Did you serve as a centurion of the first cohort?"

"I did," replied Saint Marcellus.

"What madness came over you," said Agricolanus, "that you should renounce your military oath and say such things?"

Saint Marcellus replied: "There is no madness in him who fears God."

Agricolanus said: "You did say all that is contained in the governor's proceedings?"

"I did," replied Saint Marcellus.

Agricolanus said: "You did throw down your weapons?"

"I did," replied Saint Marcellus, "for it is not proper for a Christian, who fears Christ the Lord, to fight for the troubles of this world."

5. "Since this is the case," said Agricolanus, "Marcellus' deeds must be punished in accordance with military procedure." Then he spoke as follows: "Whereas Marcellus has publicly rejected and defiled the oath of the centurion's rank in which he served, and has, according to the governor's court records, uttered certain words full of madness, we hereby decree that he be executed by the sword."

After these words were spoken, Marcellus was beheaded and thus won the martyr's palm that he desired, in the reign of our Lord Jesus Christ, who has received his martyr in peace: to him is honour, glory, valour, and power for ever. Amen.

The case of Dasius is related to us through a document that is part ideology and part court report. At the beginning, we find an account of a festival of Saturnalia that lasted for a period of thirty days. The army no doubt had its festival of Saturn lasting from the seventeenth of December to the twenty-fifth, but this account is totally out of character with army discipline, especially the part about human sacrifice. Why this outrageous tale is told is not entirely clear; possibly it had to do with the Sacian feast of the Persians as Musurillo suggested.[6] The authentic portion of this account begins at number six; one can easily see that the story about the Saturn festival has been tacked on because the sense of the narrative changes radically at this point. Now the focus is on Dasius's failure to sacrifice, an easily believable offense in the year 303 during the Great Persecution of Diocletian. Confessing in the name of the "holy Trinity," however, likely is an interpolated anachronism (8). In number eleven it appears that Christian material is added to the easily identifiable *acta* form. This martyrdom took place in the province of Moesia Inferior, modern Bulgaria, if the added information is correct.

THE MARTYRDOM OF THE SAINTLY DASIUS[7]

(Lord, have mercy!)

6. When the holy martyr Dasius had been brought by the detachment before the tribunal of the commander Bassus, Bassus looked at him and said: "What is your station and what is your name?"

The blessed Dasius answered with sincerity and openness: "I am a soldier by rank. Of my name I shall tell you, that I have the excellent one of Christian; but the name given me by my parents is Dasius."

7. Bassus the commander said: "Venerate the images of our lords the emperors, who give us peace, give us our rations, and every day show concern for our every advantage."

The blessed Dasius replied: "I have already told you and I repeat, I am a Christian, and I do not fight for any earthly king but for the king of heaven. His is the bounty I possess, I live by his favour, and I am wealthy because of his ineffable kindness."

8. The commander Bassus said: "Dasius, supplicate the holy images of our emperors, which even the barbarian nations worship and revere."

The blessed martyr Dasius said: "I confess I am a Christian as I have confessed many times before, and I obey no one else but the one undefiled and eternal God, Father, Son, and Holy Spirit, who are three in name and person but one in substance.

"So now by this triple formula I confess my faith in the holy Trinity, for strengthened by it I can quickly conquer and overthrow the Devil's madness."

9. "You forget, Dasius," said the commander Bassus, "that every man is subject to the imperial decree and to the sacred laws. Since I am sparing you, you will answer me fearlessly and without anxiety."

But Dasius, the blessed and saintly athlete of Christ, replied and said: "Do whatever has been commanded you by the impious and evil emperors. For I guard my faith which I once pledged to God to preserve, and I believe that I shall persevere firmly and unshakeably in my confession. Nor can your threats shake my resolution."

10. The commander Bassus said: "Here now, you are granted a delay in case you wish to consider in your mind how you might be able to live among us in honour."

But the blessed Dasius said: "What need is there for a delay? I have already revealed to you my intention and my resolve when I said, 'Do what you will: I am a Christian!' For, look you, as for your emperors and their honour, I spit upon it and despise it, that after the release from this life I may be able to live in that one."

11. Then the commander Bassus, after subjecting him to many torments, passed sentence that he should be beheaded. As he was going off to his glorious martyrdom, he had someone preceding him with the forbidden censer. But when they tried to force Dasius to offer sacrifice to the impure demons, picking it up in his own hands he scattered all their incense about and threw down the impious and unlawful images of the sacrilegious emperors and

trampled on them, whilst he fortified his forehead with the seal of the precious cross of Christ, by whose power he so mightily resisted the tyrant.

12. Thus the holy martyr went to his beheading on the twentieth of November, on Friday at the fourth hour, on the twenty-fourth day of the moon. Put to death by the executioner Ioannes Anicetus, he fulfilled his martyrdom in peace. The contest of the saintly Dasius took place in the city of Durostorum, under the emperors Maximian and Diocletian, and he was arraigned by the commander Bassus, while our Lord Christ Jesus was ruler in heaven, to whom is glory with Father and the Holy Spirit, now and for all ages. Amen.

Julius the Veteran died in the year 303, but it is not clear where he was when martyred; Harnack thought in Durostorum.[8] This account tells of a veteran who had reenlisted and was caught for refusing to sacrifice. Several features of the account are of interest. It seems as though Julius was a Christian in the army for some time, for precisely how long we cannot tell, and that he was involved in seven campaigns in which he fought aggressively "and never hid behind anyone." He used his service record as a good soldier to show that he was even more loyal to Christ, and perhaps also to gain respect from the judge. The way he was treated provides us a good view of the comparison between Roman and Christian religious practice. Maximus the judge was willing to make it appear as though Julius had been forced to sacrifice, just so long as he performed the rites. It did not matter in the least whether Julius "believed in" what he was doing. Julius, however, took his faith seriously in that he could not believe in Christ on the one hand and offer sacrifice on the other.

THE MARTYRDOM OF JULIUS THE VETERAN[9]

1. In the time of persecution, when the glorious ordeals which the Christians faced looked to merit the eternal promises, Julius was arrested by the prefect's staff soldiers and he was brought before the prefect Maximus.

"Who is this?" asked Maximus.

One of the staff replied: "This is a Christian who will not obey the laws."

"What is your name?" asked the prefect.

"Julius," was the reply.

"Well, what say you, Julius?" asked the prefect. "Are these allegations true?"

"Yes, they are," said Julius. "I am indeed a Christian. I do not deny that I am precisely what I am."

"You are surely aware," said the prefect, "of the emperors' edicts which order you to offer sacrifice to the gods?"

"I am aware of them," answered Julius. "But I am a Christian and cannot do what you want; for I must not lose sight of my living and true God."

2. The prefect Maximus said: "What is so serious about offering some incense and going away?"

Julius replied: "I cannot despise the divine commandments or appear unfaithful to my god. In all the twenty-seven years in which I made the mistake, so it appears, to serve foolishly in the army, I was never brought before a magistrate either as a criminal or a trouble-maker. I went on seven military campaigns, and never hid behind anyone nor was I the inferior of any man in battle. My chief never found me at fault. And now do you suppose that I, who was always found to be faithful in the past, should now be unfaithful to higher orders?"

"What military service did you have?" asked Maximus the prefect.

"I was in the army," answered Julius, "and when I had served my term I re-enlisted as a veteran. All of this time I worshipped in fear the *God who made heaven and earth* (Acts 4:24), and even to this day I show him my service."

"Julius," said Maximus the prefect, "I see that you are a wise and serious person. You shall receive a generous bonus if you will take my advice and sacrifice to the gods."

"I will not do what you wish," answered Julius, "lest I incur an eternal penalty."

"If you think it a sin," answered the prefect Maximus, "let me take the blame. I am the one who is forcing you, so that you may not give impression of having consented voluntarily. Afterwards you can go home in peace, you will pick up your ten-year bonus, and no one will ever trouble you again."

"This is the money of Satan, and neither it nor your crafty talk can deprive me of the eternal light. I cannot deny God. So, deliver sentence against me as a Christian."

3. Maximus said: "If you do not respect the imperial decrees and offer sacrifice, I am going to cut your head off."

"That is a good plan!" answered Julius. "Only I beg you, good prefect, by the welfare of your emperors, that you execute your plan and pass sentence on me, so that my prayers may be fulfilled."

"If you do not change your mind and sacrifice," said Maximus the prefect, "you will be delivered to your desires."

"If I should deserve to suffer this, I shall have eternal praise," answered Julius.

"You are being offered advice," said Maximus. "For if you endured this for the sake of the civil law, you would have eternal glory."

Julius replied: "I surely suffer for the law—but it is the divine law."

Maximus said: "You mean the law given you by a man who was crucified and died? Look how foolish you are to fear a dead man more than living emperors!"

"It was he who died for our sins (1 Cor. 15:3)," answered Julius, "in order to give us eternal life. The same man, Christ, is God and abides for ever and ever. Whoever believes in him will have eternal life (cf. John 6:47 and elsewhere), and whoever denies him will have eternal punishment."

"I counsel you out of pity," said Maximus, "that you sacrifice and continue to live with us."

"To live with you," answered Julius, "would be death for me. But, in God's sight, if I die I shall live for ever."

"Listen to me and offer the sacrifice," said Maximus, "lest I put you to death as I promised."

"I have chosen death for now," said Julius, "that I might live with the saints forever." ·

The prefect Maximus then delivered the sentence as follows: "Whereas Julius has refused to obey the imperial edicts, he is sentenced to death."

4. When he was led off to the usual spot, everyone kissed him. The blessed Julius said to them: "Let each one consider what sort of kiss this is."

There was a man named Isichius, a soldier who was a Christian, who was also being kept in prison. He said to the holy martyr: "Julius, I beg you, fulfil your promise in joy. Take the crown which the Lord has promised to give to those who believe in him (cf. Jas 1:12), and remember me, for I will follow you. Give my warmest greetings to the servant of God, our brother Valentio who has already preceded us to the Lord by his loyal confession of faith."

Julius then kissed Isichius. "Hasten, my brother, and follow me," he said. "He whom you greeted will hear your last requests."

Then he took the blindfold and bound his eyes, bent his neck, and said: "Lord Jesus Christ, I suffer this for your name. I beg you, deign to receive my spirit (cf. Acts 7:59) together with your holy martyrs."

And so the Devil's servant struck the blessed martyr with a sword and brought his life to an end, in Christ Jesus our Lord, to whom is honour and glory for ever. Amen.

The acts of Tipasius, which we will not include here, are another example of a mixture of fable and of authentic acts. He was another veteran who was martyred in 304. The grounds are the same as for other martyrs in the army at this time: refusal to sacrifice to the emperors. That is, it was after the year 303 when the demand to sacrifice had become a regular feature of army life; obviously Diocletian had extended the demand for sacrifice from the civilian to the military as well. This is exactly what one would expect, since the army was the organization responsible for conducting the sacrifice tests among the general population.[10]

After the persecutions came to an end in 313 the theme of soldiers martyred for their faith became popular for several centuries. These accounts did not display the *acta* form and are easily disqualified as unreliable sources for the persecution in the army. They are, however, valuable means of access to the common mind, and valuable sources for unlocking what was popular religious entertainment for the "average" churchman. Judging from the number of them in the *Acta Sanctorum,* one can say that such stories were well received in that some of the same themes, as in the apocryphal gospels, were repeated time and again. To illustrate how prolific were the imaginations of these people, we can take the martyrdom of the eighty-three soldiers. It had its inspiration in an inscription which read LXXXIII MIL, MIL taken for an abbreviation for *milites* ("soldiers"). Actually the MIL stood for *miliarius* meaning "mile"—a whole account of the martyrdom of a century of soldiers during the time of Diocletian had been fabricated out of a milestone indicating eighty-three miles to some place or another.[11]

Whether authentic or imaginative, all the accounts of military martyrs repeat the same theme. Soldiers got in trouble with the army because of religious policy, never on the basis of a refusal to kill or to serve in combat.

This evidence, although limited, is significant. The total absence of any motif of nonviolence or pacifism in material such as this, especially when added to what we have presented in earlier chapters, presents a serious challenge to any historical view that would depict early Christians generally as being strongly pacifist or nonviolent. The evidence as we have read it, attempting to focus our attention primarily on the everyday experience of the ordinary Christian rather than on the teaching of this or that Father, actually suggests the opposite.

NOTES

1. Herbert Musurillo, *The Acts of the Christian Martyrs* (Oxford: Oxford University Press, 1972), 240–43.

2. J. Helgeland, "Christians and the Roman Army from Marcus Aurelius to Constantine," *ANRW* 2.23.1, pp. 780–83.

3. Musurillo, *Acts*, 244–49.

4. Franz Dölger, "Sacramentum Militiae," *Antike und Christentum* 2 (1930), 268–80; G. R. Watson, *The Roman Soldier* (Ithaca, N.Y.: Cornell University Press, 1969), 50–51.

5. Musurillo, *Acts*, 250–59. Recension M, which we do not quote here, is, for our purposes, similar in all essential matters to recension N.

6. Musurillo, *Acts*, 273 n. 1.

7. Musurillo, *Acts*, 272–79. We begin our quotation at number six where the obviously authentic portion of the account begins.

8. Helgeland, "Christians and the Roman Army," 787–88.

9. Musurillo, *Acts*, 260–65.

10. Helgeland, "Christians and the Roman Army," 785–87.

11. H. Delehaye, *The Legends of the Saints*, trans. D. Attwater (New York: Fordham University Press, 1962).

10.

Eusebius[1]

If we are to understand Eusebius's position concerning the relationship between the church and military service, we must first locate him on the map of religious and political thought within the later Roman Empire. Such an approach is particularly necessary in our day because much recent historiography on the question of pacifism has not respected this context. Accordingly, once this task has been accomplished, certain problems which have concerned historians for the last century simply evaporate. Chief among these false labors is the notion that, once Constantine made Christianity the official religion of the empire, the church lost its soul. This view is more difficult to eradicate than merely pointing out that Constantine never made Christianity official. Three topics must receive attention before moving into Eusebius's view on the subject of Christians in the Roman army. The first is Eusebius's apologetic stance toward the Roman government. The second is an overview of the church's treatment of the question whether church members ought to be involved with the military, and finally, attention must be given the divine kingship model of the emperor upon which Eusebius depended.

1. It is amazing that Eusebius has not been included in the lists of the apologists. The surprise is particularly acute in that all those who used philosophy as a primary medium of argument to secure the acceptance of Christians in the Roman Empire failed in that task. It was a primary purpose of Eusebius's *Ecclesiastical History* to pour Roman facts into a Christian framework. From the first few pages onward, Eusebius argued that the success of the empire was owed to the fact that Christ was born during the administration of Octavian. Such an occurrence was no accident. The empire was the beginning of a new age, and Christ, as the Logos of God, was the breaking in of a new world to end the polytheism of previous generations. Augustus's significance was that he ended the polyarchy of previous history.[2]

2. With specific reference to military matters, Eusebius wrote loyalty in large letters throughout his work. No doubt the attack of the conservative Roman Celsus (see above, chap. 6 on Origen) had a lot to do with this response of Eusebius. For Celsus had said that, if all Romans did the same as the Christians, there would be nobody left to defend the empire against barbarian assault (Origen *Against Celsus* 8.68–69). Celsus suggested in addition that a large number of Christians in the empire might become seditious,[3] a fear which many Romans held. Tertullian, as we saw above, had also addressed that objection (*Apology* 37.3–5) by saying that, if they had a mind to do so, the Christians could burn the empire down in one night, but fortunately for the empire they would rather be killed than kill. Eusebius then amplifies the theme, begun by both Tertullian and Origen, that the church is loyal to the empire.

Eusebius, as Tertullian had also done (*Apology* 5.6; *Ad Scapulam* 4.6), referred to the event of the Thundering Legion in A.D. 173 as a way of demonstrating the loyalty of the Christians to the empire. We have already outlined (see above chap. 4 on Tertullian) the fascinating story about how the hard-pressed *Legio XII Fulminata* was miraculously delivered by a thunderstorm and lightning bolts (*Ecclesiastical History* 5.4.3–5, 7).[4] Apparently sensitive about the unusual nature of this account, Eusebius reports that this story was narrated even by those outside the faith. (Even today visitors in Rome can see three panels on the column of Marcus Aurelius that depict this incident.) Moreover, Eusebius tells us that Marcus informed the senate about the aid given by the Christians and that he asked the senate to allay the persecutions directed against the Christians. This part is not likely; we know that Marcus approved the action against the Christians in Lyons-Vienne four years later. Apparently Eusebius also knew that not everything was right in his story, for he ascribes this outbreak of persecution to Verus, Marcus's brother and co-emperor who died in 169, eight years before. Even in matters of chronology, Eusebius was apologetic.

This episode is typical of the ways in which Eusebius treats all his church history in an apologetic fashion. Here are some of his important points: (1) Christians are loyal to the empire. (2) Their loyalty has positive consequences for the empire. (3) Good emperors favor the church while bad or incompetent ones, such as Verus, cause the church grief. (4) There was no criticism of those Christians serving in this legion or any other. Eusebius said nothing which might dissuade us from assuming that Christians fought just as effectively as any other Roman soldier. The *XII Fulminata* did recruit heavily in areas known at that time to have many Christians, although we must honestly doubt that it was composed entirely of Christians. Nevertheless, Eusebius wrote that this was a completely Christian legion, and that probably is what most Christians thought when they read him.

At this point, those supporting the position that the first three centuries of Christianity were pacifist would likely say that Eusebius had compromised an essential teaching of the church. They would say that it was for the sake of courting the favor of Rome that Eusebius betrayed the faith. In sorting out the difference, a great deal of evidence can be brought forward that supports Eusebius's position over against a pacifist interpretation.

Eusebius does not mention in all of his work any general theory of pacifism in the church as a whole. There is in fact little significant evidence that there was one. Among the flimsy data available to support the opposite opinion, the witness of Origen stands out; but his position, especially in its aftereffects, was quite ambiguous, as we have seen above. First, it would be difficult to find a church father who at some point or other did not say he abhorred war. Who does not? Even some of the most violent generals have said they detest the waste of battle. Second, the statements which say that it is wrong to kill, and they are indeed frequently found in the literature, are quite general in nature. Hippolytus and Tertullian excepted, they are rarely in a military context. In fact, general prohibitions against killing prove just as easily the opposite of what pacifist interpretations would like to establish. Second, if one assumes that it is a waste of time to prohibit what is not taking place, and that repeated prohibitions of a particular crime usually indicate that that crime is widespread, then there may have been far more violence among early Christians than we had previously thought. There is actually a record of one unrepentant Christian murderer.[5] Most of the passages prohibiting killing could refer as easily to murder in a domestic context. Third, some pacifist historians argue that there was no need to prohibit induction into the legions because the commands of Jesus about turning the other cheek and walking the extra mile were still ringing clearly in the Christians' ears. If one were to consult the apocryphal gospels, however, a quite different picture emerges. If Christians were so intent on following Jesus' dicta in every respect, what accounts for all those interesting stories about Jesus killing everyone who irritates him? What was the source and who were the tellers of stories like the one in which a representative of the parents in Nazareth comes to Mary and Joseph to tell them they should keep their child at home, for those who anger him die (*The*

Infancy Gospel of Thomas; see above, chap. 7 on apocryphal gospels). It is important to know that these writings, crass and bizarre as they are, were the products of a rich oral tradition. Sometimes the same stories, usually the ones about Jesus killing his playmates, appear in several of these gospels.

As we saw above, the problem of Christians entering the Roman army was not pacifism but army religion. Eusebius must have understood this too, although apologetic considerations prevented him from reopening this issue. In book 7.15 of the *Ecclesiastical History,* Eusebius relates the story of Marinus who, during the reign of Gallienus, intended to receive promotion to centurion. Other soldiers in the unit made an issue of his Christianity and his inability to sacrifice to the emperor, perhaps a way by which the soldier next in line could remove competition. From the account (see above, chap. 9 on military martyrs), it is clear that Marinus had worked his way up through the ranks and intended to stay in the army. A bishop appeared at his trial and took Marinus away for a time, meanwhile presenting him a sword and a Bible and asking him to choose one or the other. Marinus chose the Bible and was martyred. This account points to a sharp conflict between Christianity and army religion. But Eusebius did not comment on it other than to recopy it into his history.[6]

3. To turn to the theme of the divine king, we see Eusebius at all points fitting Constantine into this framework. In classical views, it was the emperor who made the connection between heaven and earth. In so doing, the king or emperor brought salvation, interpreted as a series of material and social blessings, into the empire. Eusebius elaborates this theme by viewing the emperor as the ensoulment of the cosmic order: the emperor is to the state as God is to the world, a cosmic liturgy as Chesnut describes it.[7] In Philo's thinking, the divine connection is the reason a Jew could not venerate the Roman emperor. Eusebius, like Philo, was a monotheist. So when Constantine began wiping out the other Augusti and Caesars to become sole ruler of the empire, Eusebius breathed more easily theologically. Constantine, with each kill—Maxentius, then Licinius—became increasingly closer to the earthly icon of God's monarchy. Eusebius used biblical imagery to augment the understanding of the Roman divine king. When Maxentius with many of his bodyguard fell off Milvian Bridge, at that time a pontoon bridge, and drowned, the image which came to Eusebius was that of Moses drowning the Pharaoh's troops in the Red Sea.

The divinity of Constantine appears in the *Ecclesiastical History* as an apocalyptic phenomenon. Eusebius believed that Constantine's coming to power meant that the end times were close at hand and he believed that the world had lived out most of its history. Concomitant with this turn in world affairs was the apocalyptic destruction of demons. It was the demons, after all, that had entered into the wicked emperors who had been the persecutors of Christianity. So it was that the demons served both a theological and a political function particularly by helping Eusebius admit that emperors had set a precedent by persecuting Christians. It was not emperors but demons who had caused all the trouble. In typical apocalyptic fashion, God gets back at all who had persecuted the chosen, beginning with Herod whose illness Eusebius copied in every delicious detail from Josephus. When Constantine becomes violent and victorious he is only doing God's work.

This is the picture Eusebius develops concerning the final battle with Licinius. In every way it becomes a religious battle to decide whether the Christian God or that of the Romans shall be victorious. Everywhere Constantine relentlessly conquers because he is a "friend of God." Licinius is doomed; he has gone mad and turned against the church which formerly he supported.[8] It made no difference to Eusebius that Licinius had been a supporter of the Christians only to be betrayed by them when it was clear that Constantine intended to conquer the entire empire. There is not the slightest sense of tragedy as Eusebius recounts the destruction of Licinius's army. The Christian apocalyptic crusade had been born and anything in its path was to be swept away in a storm of fire.

The Synod of Arles

One can see that Eusebius was ecstatic at Constantine'ᵣ rise to power. But what of Christians in the West? Their response to Constantine was to aid him by keeping Christian soldiers in the army. In August 314 the Synod of Arles (an important Roman city near the mouth of the Rhone) stated in canon 3: "Concerning those, who throw down their arms in time of peace, we have decreed that they should be kept from communion."[9] The phrase, "in time of peace" has caused a great deal of controversy because even historians who were not pacifists often accepted pacifist assumptions about the early church. They expected to see soldiers throwing down their arms in time of *war*, not peace. On that account they have questioned whether the text we have is accurate, but there is no evidence that it has been corrupted.

The canon refers to those soldiers who have actually disarmed themselves in peacetime. The military martyrs and those inclined to follow their example are the ones meant, most likely. It was the martyr Marcellus who literally threw off his sword belt. Since all these soldiers had problems with idolatry, it is the idolatrous atmosphere in the army that stands in the background of canon 3.

Even though Constantine had come to power there is no reason for us to believe that the nature of the army had changed overnight to an organization which would make Christians feel at home. We have seen in connection with the festivals retained from republican times that the Roman army, like most armies, was conservative. Much later Ambrose complained, for example, that the army still used the eagle to lead its troops. A commander could not, in one swoop, remove the traditional emblems and rituals which were essential to the army's self-identification and morale.

The time of Constantine's accession to power is when we would expect to have some record of the church's objection to having Christians serve in his armies. If the pacifist view of early church history is correct, if pacifism was as basic to the church's attitude as that view claims, this objection surely would have been given voice. There is, however, not one word which would indicate any controversy whatsoever. Given Constantine's ambitions for power, it would have been strange indeed if he had chosen to befriend a religious community known for a refusal to fight for the empire, or for having members who refused to enlist in his armies.

NOTES

1. See the fuller treatment in J. Helgeland, "Christians and the Roman Army from Marcus Aurelius to Constantine," *ANRW* 2.23.1, pp. 760–62, 812–15.

2. G. F. Chesnut, *The First Christian Histories* (Paris: Gabriel Beauchesne, 1977), 99–101.

3. R. M. Grant, *From Augustus to Constantine* (New York: Harper & Row, 1970), 93.

4. See Helgeland, "Christians and the Roman Army," 766–74.

5. J. Stevenson, *A New Eusebius* (London: SPCK, 1968), 308.

6. See Helgeland, "Christians and the Roman Army," 762–64.

7. Chesnut, *First Christian Histories,* chap. 6.

8. Eusebius *Life of Constantine* 2.3–4.

9. Stevenson, *A New Eusebius*, 322; C. J. Hefele, *Histoire des Conciles,* trans. H. Leclercq (Paris: Letouzey, 1907) 1:282.

11.

Ambrose and Augustine

In the late fourth and early fifth centuries, Christianity made a transition from toleration to establishment. The traditional Roman cult was deprived of state support and the emperors looked to the Christian God as the guarantor of the fortunes of Rome. Ambrose, bishop of Milan, responded by applying scriptural images of the Israelite kings to the Roman emperors. Augustine of Hippo developed a theory of the complementarity of the earthly and heavenly cities which legitimated the waging of war by Christian rulers. Two incidents illustrate the change in the social situation of the church and the corresponding development in theology: the victory of Theodosius I over the Western usurper Eugenius in September 394, and the career of Boniface, the governor of Africa during the 420s.

One of the issues that came to decision in Theodosius's defeat of Eugenius at the River Frigidus on 5 September 394 was state support for the traditional Roman religion.[1] Although he protected and promoted Christianity, Constantine did not disturb the privileges of the state religion: funding of sacrifices and of the Vestal Virgins, the presence of the Altar of Victory in the Senate House, and the exemption of religious officers from public burdens. His son Constantius (337–61) at one time prohibited the practice of the cult and removed the Altar of Victory but subsequently reversed himself. Julian (361–63) promoted the traditional pagan religion and increased the support for its officials. This arrangement was disturbed by neither Jovinian (363–64) nor Valentinian (364–75). Under the influence of Ambrose, the young emperor Gratian undertook a program of disestablishment. Upon his accession in 375, he refused the traditional title of *Pontifex Maximus*. In 382, he reassigned the revenues dedicated to the cult, revoked the exemptions and removed the Altar of Victory. Ambrose was instrumental in maintaining these policies by opposing a series of appeals from the traditional party in the Senate to Valentinian II and Theodosius.

In May 392, the young Valentinian II died under unexplained circumstances and Eugenius was set up as Western emperor. Although he was a professing Christian, the pagan party in the Senate rallied to Eugenius's support and was rewarded by the restoration of support for its religion. Attempts to secure the support of the Christian bishops through gifts were less successful. Ambrose, for example, withdrew from Milan in order to avoid communion with Eugenius. The bishops waited for the reaction of the Eastern emperor Theodosius to these developments.

When Theodosius finally moved his army westward in the spring of 394, the pagan revival was in full swing. Pagan oracles foretold the defeat of Theodosius and the early demise of Christianity. Eugenius went out to meet him under the standard of Hercules and set up statues of Jupiter to guard the Alpine passes. Theodosius easily forced the mountain passage, but he had more difficulty with the army of Eugenius on the plain of the River Frigidus just east of Aquileia. In the first day of battle, 5 September 394, he lost heavily. When he renewed the attack on the following day, however, a strong wind suddenly came down from the mountains in the face of Eugenius's forces. This gale propelled the arrows and javelins thrown by Theodosius's army and turned back those of his enemy. In addition, the Gothic auxiliaries that had been sent to cut off Theodosius's retreat defected and joined the battle on his side. Theodosius's victory was complete, and Ambrose looked on it as clearly God's work:

25. Thus, "The spear of sinners will enter their own heart," he says, "and their bows will be broken" [Ps 37:15]. Just as the peace in which God's servants bless will return to them from those who refuse it, so the malice from which sinners try to harm the just person will redound to their own destruction. They will be cut down by wounds from their own missiles. It sometimes happens that thrown weapons are flung back on those who launched them.

This happened, in fact, during the latest war. Faithless and sacrilegious men challenged one who placed his trust in the Lord. They attempted to deprive him of his dominion and they threatened the churches of the Lord with savage persecutions. Suddenly a wind sprang up; it ripped the rebels' shields out of their hands and cast all the javelins and missiles back on the sinner's army. Their opponents had not yet attacked but already they could not sustain the assault of the wind and were cut down by their own weapons. What is more, the wounds in their spirits were deeper than those in their bodies; they lost heart when they realized that God was fighting against them.

They had gone forth with a challenge; from the quivers of their hearts they had drawn the poisoned arrows of infidelity against the Christian people. Then their impiety was turned back on their own heads. Their unfaithfulness caused divisions among themselves. The Lord broke up the trap they had laid for his faithful ones. Thus not only were they unable to harm the devout but they were deprived of their own auxiliaries and their support went over to their opponent.

How much better it would have been if they had never unsheathed the sword, had never uttered the irreverent words. If every person must give an account of even an idle word, how much more will he atone by horrible punishments for sacrilegious speeches. (Ambrose *Exposition of Psalm* 35 25)

The Christian authors who recounted this victory enhanced the narrative in various ways to clarify the divine intervention that crushed the pagan revolt against the Christian emperor. Christian prophecy was vindicated and pagan divinization discredited through the opposing predictions of victory by the Christian anchorite, John of Lycopolis, and the pagan priest Flavian. At the shrine of John the Baptist where Theodosius had prayed upon leaving Constantinople, a demoniac rushed in at the moment of victory and accused the saint of destroying his armies. The pagan offerings at the Altar of Victory failed Eugenius; Theodosius's total reliance on Christ was rewarded. Theodosius refused to heed his generals' advice to withdraw after the first day; he asserted the cross of Christ must not appear weaker than the image of Hercules. A prayer of Theodosius for God's intervention in the midst of battle was credited with inspiring the whole army and bringing the Goths over to his side. A night vision of John the Evangelist and Philip the Apostle that Theodosius and a soldier in the rank independently beheld before the second day's battle assured Theodosius of their support. The clearest sign of divine intervention was, of course, the wind. Ambrose explained that the tempest itself effected the victory before Theodosius even attacked. For Augustine, Theodosius triumphed more by prayer than by the sword.[2]

Ambrose, Augustine, and the Christian historians viewed the revolt of Eugenius and the victory of Theodosius as a struggle between Christ and the demons. The cause of Christ and that of Theodosius were identified. God had intervened to vindicate his champion just as he had in order to bring victory to Moses, Joshua, and David. When Theodosius died some four months later, Ambrose proclaimed that he was glorified in heaven with Gratian and Valentinian while Eugenius and their other enemies were condemned in hell for their revolt.[3]

The second instance to be considered involved Augustine and the governor of Roman Africa, Boniface. As a military officer, Boniface served in Europe before being sent to Africa in 417. Augustine dealt with him in the suppression of Donatist violence and seems to have been deeply attached to him. Boniface was guarding the southern border of Numidia, Augustine's province, when his wife died. Broken by sorrow, Boniface proposed to abandon his military career and take up the monastic life. Augustine wrote to him and in 421, at the age of sixty-seven, undertook an overland journey of more than six hundred kilometers to visit him. In an extended private interview, he persuaded Boniface to serve God as a soldier in pacifying the barbarians and protecting the church.[4]

Augustine's letter to Boniface establishes the Christian military vocation on the twin commands of love of God and neighbor.[5] Like every Christian life, its moving force is the Spirit's gift of charity and its end is the heavenly peace. Scriptural citations from both Testaments remove any doubt of the compatibility of the military and the Christian calling. Because Boniface was attracted to the monastic life, Augustine demonstrated the similarity and complementarity of the two vocations. In prayer, the monk fights for the soldier against invisible enemies. In battle, the soldier labors for the monk against visible barbarians. If the whole world were Christian, each would find the struggle easier, but presumably still necessary. The celibate chastity and withdrawal from worldly affairs which the monk practices place him in a higher rank before God. The soldier, however, must practice conjugal chastity, sobriety, and temperance to prevent his being overcome by passion and ruled by greed and ambition.

Augustine urged Boniface to recognize his bodily strength and military skill as a divine gift to be dedicated to the service of God's people. The earthly peace that foreshadows that eternal peace of the kingdom of heaven must be the soldier's sole aim—to be attained by violence in war and mercy in the victory.

2. This is what I can say in a short space: "Love the Lord your God in all your heart, all your soul, and all your power; love your neighbor as yourself" [Mt 22:37, 39]. This is the summary which the Lord gave when he spoke on earth in the Gospel: "The whole Law and Prophets depend on these two commands" [Mt 22:40]. Grow in this love every day by prayer and good works. The Lord both commanded and gave this love to you; by his help may it be nourished and increased in you, so that by reaching its own fullness it may perfect you as well. This, indeed, is the charity which "is poured forth in our hearts through the Holy Spirit who is given to us," as the Apostle says [Rom 5:5]. Of this he says, "The fullness of the law is charity" [Rom 13:10]. This is the charity through which faith works, so that he says again, "Neither circumcision nor uncircumcision is worth anything but only faith which works through love." [Gal 5:6]

4. Do not suppose that a person who serves in the army cannot be pleasing to God. The holy David, a soldier, was given high praise by our Lord. Many of

the just men of his time were also soldiers. Another soldier, the centurion, said to the Lord, "I am not worthy to have you enter under my roof but only speak a word and my servant will be healed. I, indeed, am a man subject to authority and have soldiers under me. I say to one, 'Go' and he goes; to another, 'Come' and he comes; to my servant 'Do this' and he does it." The Lord said to him, "Amen, I say to you, I have not found such faith in Israel" [Mt 8:8–10]. There was another soldier, Cornelius, to whom an angel was sent to say, "Cornelius, your alms are recognized and your prayers are heard." Then he told him to send for the blessed Apostle Peter and to hear from him what he should do. He sent another devout soldier to bring the apostle to him (Acts 10:1–8, 30–33]. Soldiers came to John to be baptized, to that forerunner of the Lord and friend of the bridegroom, of whom the Lord himself said, "Among those born of woman, none greater than John the Baptist has arisen" [Mt 11:11]. When the soldiers asked him what to do, he replied, "Do not extort money from anyone; do not bring false charges against anyone; be satisfied with your pay" [Lk 3:12–14]. He certainly was not forbidding them to serve in the army when he commanded them to be satisfied with their pay.

5. Those who abandon all the affairs of this age and then serve the Lord in fully continent chastity certainly have a higher place before him. Still, the Apostle says that, "Each one has his own proper gift from God: one this way and another that" [1 Cor 7:7]. Thus others fight for you against invisible enemies by praying; you work for them against visible barbarians by fighting. We could wish that everyone shared the one faith since then the work would be less and the devil with his angels would be conquered more easily. In this age, however, the citizens of the Heavenly Kingdom are driven about by trials among the misguided and irreligious. Thus they are trained and proven like gold in the furnace. We must not desire to live with the holy and just alone before the appropriate time, so that when that time comes, we may deserve to attain it.

6. When you are arming yourself for battle, therefore, let this thought be foremost in your mind: even your bodily strength is God's gift. Think about God's gift in this way and do not use it against God. Once you have given your word, you must keep it to the opponent against whom you wage war and all the more to your friend for whom you fight. You must always have peace as your objective and regard war as forced upon you, so that God may free you from this necessity and preserve you in peace. Peace is not sought in order to stir up war; war is waged to secure the peace. You must, therefore, be a peacemaker even in waging war so that by your conquest you may lead those you subdue to the enjoyment of peace. "Blessed are the peacemakers," says the Lord, "for they shall be called children of God" [Mt 5:9]. How sweet is human peace for the temporal prosperity of mortals; yet how much the sweeter is that eternal peace for the eternal salvation of the angels. May it be necessity, therefore, not your own desire, which destroys your attacking enemy. As you respond with ferocity to the rebelling and resisting, so do you owe compassion to the defeated and captured, especially when you no longer fear a disturbance of the peace.

7. Let married chastity be the decoration of your way of life, let temperance and simplicity adorn it. How disgraceful it would be for someone whom no man conquers to fall victim to lust or for one who is not overcome by the

sword to be subverted by wine. If the riches of this age are lacking, they should not be pursued in this world by evil deeds; if they are possessed, let them be kept in heaven by good works. Their acquisition should not lift up nor should their passing break the strong, Christian spirit. Let us think instead of what the Lord said, "Where your treasure is, there will your heart be too" [Mt 6:21]. Certainly, when we hear the call to lift up our hearts, the answer you know we make should not be given in vain. (Augustine *Letter* 189.2, 4–7)

Boniface seems to have been initially convinced, to have dedicated himself to a life of continence and military service. Subsequently, however, he fell victim to ambition and lust: he entered an advantageous marriage and may have taken concubines. His fortunes rose and he was named Count of Africa. Then a rival betrayed him; he revolted against the emperor and held off the army sent to reduce him to submission. The land he was to protect was devastated by civil war: the raids of the barbarians he had earlier held in check, and the invasion of the Vandals, for which he seems to have been in part responsible.

Augustine wrote Boniface again to admonish him to attend to his eternal salvation.[6] In his letter, all the problems that the people suffer are traced to the lust and ambition that Boniface failed to hold in check. Ruled by these passions, he cannot control his own subordinates. In order to retain their loyalty, he must tolerate their greed and injustice. Here Augustine demonstrated the devastation and suffering of a people whose ruler has been overcome by the invisible demons and subjected to passion. Had Boniface been true to his Christian vocation, Augustine implied, peace might have been maintained in Africa:

5. What shall I say about the many great evils, matters of general knowledge, in which you have been involved since your marriage? You are a Christian; you have a heart; you fear God. Consider for yourself the things I would prefer not to mention and you will realize how enormous are the evils for which you should do penance. I believe that the Lord will have mercy on you and save you from the present dangers so that you can do penance as you should. You must listen to what is written in Holy Scripture, "Do not be slow to turn to the Lord; do not put it off from one day to the next." [Sir 5:7]

You claim that your cause is just. I am no judge of that, since I cannot hear both sides. Whatever your case might be, and there is no need to hear and debate it, can you stand before God and deny that you would never have come to such a state unless you loved the goods of this world? As a servant of God, the way we knew you before, you should have completely disregarded these things and considered them worthless. When they were offered, you should have accepted them and used them for God's service. When they were refused or placed in your care, you should not have pursued them in a way which would lead to the present situation. As it is, because these worthless things are loved, many evil things have been done for your sake, however few you may have done yourself. Similarly, because things which do only brief, if any, harm are feared, those are done which cause eternal harm.

6. Let me say something about just one of these. Who does not see that a lot of men have joined you to protect your power and your safety. They may all be completely loyal to you and you may not have to fear betrayal from any of them. Still, through you these men hope to acquire those goods which they too love in a worldly way and not for God's sake. As a result, are you now forced to satisfy in others those greedy desires which you should have restrained and repressed in yourself? To accomplish this, many things displeasing to God must be done. Even then, these desires are not really satisfied. It would be much easier to restrain them in those who love God than ever to satisfy them in those who love this world. This is why Holy Scripture says, "Do not love this world or the things in this world. If anyone loves this world, the Father's love is not in him. Everything in this world is the concupiscence of the flesh, the concupiscence of the eyes, and the ambition of this age, which is not from the Father but from the world. This world passes away and its concupiscence passes with it. The one who does God's will endures forever, just as God endures forever" [1 Jn 2:15–17]. Think about all those armed men whose greed must be supported, whose ferocity is feared, who love this world. When can you hope, not to satisfy since this would be impossible, but even to allay their concupiscence in a limited way, in order to prevent the further destruction of everything? Can you accomplish this without doing what God forbids and threatens to punish? As a result, you realize that so much has already been destroyed that the pillagers have trouble finding even worthless things to carry off.

7. What can I say about the devastation of Africa which the African barbarians carry out without resistance? You are involved in your own problems and take no steps to prevent this disaster. Back when Boniface was a Tribune with only a few allies, he maintained the peace by attacking and driving out all these peoples. Who would have believed, who would have fears, once he was appointed Count of the Household and of Africa, that these barbarians would have attempted so much, advanced so far, laid waste and carried off so much, would have reduced so many populated areas to ruins? Who did not say that if you took on the power of a count, these African barbarians would not only be subdued but would even pay tribute to the Roman Empire? How differently people's hopes have turned out. I should not speak to you about this any more, for you can think of more than I can say. (Augustine *Letter* 220.5–7)

Boniface did manage to come to an understanding with the empire and regain his office. He was charged with the defense of the weakened land against the invasion of the Vandals. In June 430, he fell back on the fortified town of Hippo Regius. At the end of August, the third month of Genseric's fourteen-month siege, the town's bishop, Augustine, passed over to eternal peace. Boniface was killed in battle in Italy a few years later.

These two incidents and the ways in which Christian authors dealt with them give rise to a number of considerations. First, these bishops accepted war as a part of the sinful human condition and believed that the Christian soldier could be an agent cooperating in God's providential governance of the world. Augustine explicitly distinguished the Christian soldier serving God from the sinful conqueror whose evil God uses for his own good purposes but whose sin he then punishes.

The objective of the Christian soldier must always be peace. He must preserve it by opposing the aggressor and pardoning the vanquished. The proper exercise of coercive power requires a virtue and self-control that rival those of the monk. The soldier who falls captive to ambition, greed, and lust, who violates his allegiance or does not keep his word to an enemy will do the devil's own destructive work.

As these instances make clear, the social situation of Christianity had changed. Devoted Christians were to be found in positions of responsibility in the imperial government; these men judged themselves bound, as Augustine asserted, to serve God in their official capacity by enforcing his laws and protecting his church. Moreover, they were advised by bishops from their own social class who understood the opportunities and the limits of the exercise of political power. Under Theodosius and his successors Christianity became the established religion of the empire. Pagan practice was prohibited, and even heretical and schismatic forms of Christianity were forbidden.

In this situation, the scriptural categories and images of the Israelite monarchy could be applied to the Christian Roman Empire. Precisely this development may be observed in Ambrose's dealings with Theodosius. Recalling the example of David, he urged the emperor to repent of his sin in ordering the massacre at Thessalonica. He asserted that the usurpers who challenged the Christian emperor were defeated in war and then eternally punished by God.[7] Augustine was more cautious about civil war, although he did seem to regard the barbarians as a demonic force. In fact, of course, both bishops were primarily concerned with the peace and prosperity of the church; the power of the empire was a resource put at their disposal by God.

Still, the situation did call for some theory of the significance of war and the value of earthly peace for the empire, for the human society that was not identified with the church. In three of his writings, Augustine dealt with this question. At the end of his life, in *On the City of God,* he attempted a comprehensive treatment of earthly peace and of the Christian's responsibility for it.

Augustine first attended to the question of war and peace in his response to the Manichee Faustus, which was written in 397, shortly after his episcopal consecration.[8] Faustus attacked the God of Israel on, among other grounds, his having commanded war. This, he argued, was clearly contrary to the pacifist teaching of Jesus which the Manichees followed. Augustine replied that two sets of goods must be recognized as gifts of God: the necessities of earthly life and the joys of heaven. The wars of the OT and the victories of Christian princes like Theodosius show that temporal goods and the peace in which they are enjoyed are controlled by God. The martyrdom of Christ and his disciples, like those of the OT prophets, witness that earthly goods are to be abandoned for heavenly ones.

War itself, Augustine asserted, is a neutral action that may be performed for an appropriate reason by the proper person. The deaths of people who are to die eventually is an issue for the coward, not for the religious person. The evil of warfare lies in the evil passions that may be involved: the lust for domination, the ferocity of rebellion, savagery, and cruelty. To resist just these sorts of evils and to secure the safety of the people, God or a human ruler may wage war. The soldier whose engagement in battle is ruled not by evil passion but by loyalty to the proper authority does good, even if his ruler acts wrongly.

73. This eternal law, which commands that the natural order be preserved and forbids any disturbance of it, places some actions in a middle position so that human presumption in undertaking them is rightly blamed but obedience in carrying them out is justly praised. In the natural order, who acts and under whose direction makes a significant difference. If Abraham had himself decided to sacrifice his son, he could not have been anything but deranged and terrible. Acting on God's command, however, he showed himself faithful and trustworthy.

74. Therefore, even human harshness, accompanied by a vicious and perverse desire to misconstrue right actions, should grasp the great difference between indulging human presumption or greed and obeying the commands of God who knows what, when, and whom should be tolerated or commanded, what and who should act or suffer. If this can be understood, then the wars which Moses waged will cause neither surprise nor shock. In these wars, Moses was obediently following the divine command; he was not raging wildly. Nor was God acting savagely in commanding them; he was repaying their due to those who deserved it and frightening those who should have been.

What, indeed is wrong with war? That people die who will eventually die anyway so that those who survive may be subdued in peace? A coward complains of this but it does not bother religious people. No, the true evils in warfare are the desire to inflict damage, the cruelty of revenge, disquiet and implacability of spirit, the savagery of rebellion, the lust for domination, and other such things. Indeed, often enough good men are commanded by God or a lawful ruler to wage war precisely in order to punish these things in the face of violent resistance. In the course of human affairs, proper order sometimes forces the good either to command this sort of thing or rightly to obey such a command. Otherwise, when soldiers came to John to be baptized and asked him, "What should we do?," he would have told them: give up your weapons, leave the service, do not hit, wound, or disable anyone. He knew, however, that in doing these things in military service, they acted as enforcers of the law and defenders of public safety, not as murderers or avengers of private wrongs. For this reason, he told them, "Do not extort money from anyone; do not bring false charges against anyone; be satisfied with your pay" [Lk 3:12–14]. Since, however, the Manichees have made a habit of open attacks on John, they should note that the Lord Jesus Christ directed that these wages be paid to Caesar which John told the soldiers to accept as adequate. "Pay to Caesar what belongs to Caesar and to God what belongs to God" [Mt 22:21]. These taxes are paid in order to provide the soldier's wages which are necessary for war. Moreover, when the centurion said, "I indeed am a man subject to authority and have soldiers subject to me. I say to one, 'Go,' and he goes; to another, 'Come,' and he comes," the Lord praised his faith. He did not order him to abandon military service. At this point, a discussion of just and unjust wars would take too long and is unnecessary.

75. When humans undertake war, the person responsible and the reasons for acting are quite important. The natural order which is directed to peace among mortals requires that the ruler take counsel and initiate war; once war has been commanded, the soldiers should serve in it to promote the general peace and safety. No one must ever question the rightness of a war which is waged on God's command, since not even that which is undertaken from human greed can cause any real harm either to the incorruptible God or to any of his holy ones. God commands war to drive out, to crush or to subjugate the pride of mortals. Suffering war exercises the patience of his saints, humbles them and helps them to accept his fatherly correction. No one has any power over them unless it is given from above. All power comes from God's command or permission. Thus a just man may rightly fight for the order of civil peace even if he serves under the command of a ruler who is himself irreligious. What he is commanded to do is either clearly not contrary or not clearly contrary to God's precept. The evil of giving the command might make the king guilty but the order of obedience would keep the soldier innocent. How much more innocently, therefore, might a person engage in war when he is commanded to fight by God, who can never command anything improperly, as anyone who serves him cannot fail to realize.

76. They (the Manichees) might think that God could not have given a command to wage war because the Lord Jesus Christ later said, "I say to you, do not resist evil; if anyone strikes your right cheek, give him your left" [Mt 5:39]. They should understand, however, that this is a readiness of the heart, not the body. The heart is the holy seat of virtue, its dwelling place even in those just ancient fathers of ours. The ordered sequence of events and distinction of the ages require, however, that it should first have been made clear that earthly goods, including human kingdoms and victories over the enemy, belong to the power and the judgment of the one true God, not to the idols and demons to whom the city of the evil which has spread over the earth prays for them. For this reason, the Old Testament used earthly promises to conceal the

Kingdom of Heaven and keep it in shadow until the proper time for it to be revealed. When the fullness of time came and the New Testament, which had been covered by the old figures was unveiled, unambiguous witness had already pointed out that other life, for whose sake this life should be disregarded, and that other kingdom, for whose sake the hostility of all earthly states should be born in great patience. Similarly, God was pleased to confirm this through the confession, suffering and death of those who are called martyrs, which means witness in Latin. From heaven, Christ called Saul, changed him from being a wolf, and sent him like a sheep among wolves. Such a large number of martyrs sprang up, however, that if Christ had chosen to gather them into an army, to equip and aid them in battle as he had helped the Hebrew patriarchs, what people could have withstood them, what kingdom would have survived? In order to give clear witness to the truth which teaches that God is to be served not for temporal happiness in this life but for eternal happiness after it, what is popularly considered misfortune should be born and endured for the sake of that happiness.

In the fullness of time, the Son of God, made from a woman, made under the law to redeem those under the law, made from the seed of David according to the flesh, sends his disciples as sheep in the midst of wolves and warns them not to fear those who kill the body but cannot kill the soul. He promises to renew the integrity of the body, even to restore their hair. He orders Peter's sword back into its sheath. He restores the ear cut off the enemy to its original condition. He says he could summon legions of angels to destroy his enemies, were he not called to drink the cup which his Father's will had given. He drinks it and passes it to the followers. He reveals the virtue of patience by his precept and confirms it by his example. "For this, God raised him from the dead and gave him a name above every name, so that at the name of Jesus every knee should bend, heavenly, earthly and infernal, and every tongue confess Jesus Lord in the glory of God the Father" [Phil 2:9, 11]. The patriarchs and prophets reigned on this earth, therefore, so that it might be shown that such kingdoms are given and taken away by God. The apostles and martyrs did not rule here in order to show that the Kingdom of Heaven should be preferred. The first waged wars as kings to show that even that sort of victory comes from God's will. The second were killed without resisting to teach that to die for faith in the Truth is a better victory. Of course, even in the earlier time, the prophets knew how to die for the Truth, as the Lord said, "From the blood of Abel down to the blood of Zachary" [Mt 23:35]. The psalm prophesied of Christ, our peace, under the figure of Solomon, whose name means peacemaker in Latin, "All the kings of the earth will do him homage and all nations will serve him" [Ps 71:11]. Once this had begun to be fulfilled, Christian emperors who put full religious trust in Christ have also obtained a most glorious victory over irreligious opponents whose hope was in the worship of idols and demons. The prophecies of the demons deceived the one while the predictions of the saints strengthened the other. There are generally known proofs of this and some have already recorded it in writing. (Augustine *Against Faustus* 22.73–76)

Some twenty years later, Augustine responded to an inquiry from Boniface about the propriety of enforcing the imperial laws which required the Donatist schismatics to rejoin the unity of the Catholic church.[9] Augustine explained that the circumstances under which the imperial decree had been enacted convinced him that the emperor was acting under God's influence. The emperor has the responsibility for maintaining peace within the empire and a Christian ruler should suppress a schism in the church, which is a rebellion against his Lord, in the same way he would deal with insurrection in the empire. Christ himself established the precedent for the use of coercive force in religion by his conversion of Paul and the compelling of the wedding guests in the parable of Luke 14:16–23.

About 425, Augustine wrote his fullest consideration of war and peace in book 19 of *On the City of God*.[10] He had earlier defined the two cities in opposition to each other by love of God and of self, charity and pride. So defined, these cities were not visible social institutions. The Roman Empire in its pagan period and the Christian church in its pristine purity might have served as symbols of the two cities. Augustine had argued during the Donatist controversy, however, that the visible church was a mixed body, containing both good and evil. Similarly, he recognized the service offered to God by the Christian emperor and his officials through their political power. At first, he exhorted these men to remain in government in order to protect and provide for the church. Eventually, however, he had to develop an understanding of the religious significance of civil society itself.

Through the notion of peace, Augustine was able to relate church and state as complementary and intermingled peoples. The true and fullest peace is the eternal joy of the Kingdom of Heaven. That peace is foreshadowed in the peace sought by the earthly city: the enjoyment of the necessities of temporal life in the tranquility of order. The citizens of the earthly city seek this peace for its own sake and have no hope beyond it. Although this peace is limited, it does satisfy a deep and universal longing of the human spirit. For its sake, peoples are joined together by a common language, laws, and social institutions. The citizens of the heavenly city share this desire and strive for earthly peace, although they subordinate it to the fuller heavenly peace.

Christians will engage in war to secure the earthly peace and will suffer war as a means to heavenly peace. They will feel the burden of war since it arises from human sinfulness and will engage in it with sadness to right wrongs and to secure peace. Christians will identify with a particular nation of people in a limited way. They recognize that a variety of languages, cultures, and laws may be apt means for earthly peace and harmony. Hence, they will resist only those laws and institutions, whether foreign or domestic, that impede the service and worship of the true God.

In this analysis, Augustine recognized the legitimacy of earthly, temporal peace and the role of the Christian in working for it. He subordinated temporal peace only to the eternal peace, not to the promotion of the good of the church. The state's claim on the Christian was also limited by the goal of temporal peace. It may not hinder the quest for eternal peace nor may it assert its own social institutions as the only appropriate means to that peace.

Underlying this view of war and peace are two assumptions about the bodily condition of humanity. First, although Augustine gradually came to a fuller appreciation of the value of temporal goods, he insisted that these must be subordinated to the goods of the soul. The loss of temporal goods could be approved as a means of attaining some eternal purpose. Thus, Augustine asserts that God wages war to perfect his chosen and to punish sinners. He accomplishes his purpose by controlling the vicious will of the Christian. Second, Augustine believed that bodily death is a punishment imposed by God for the common sin of all humanity in Adam. No one dies an innocent and undeserved death, not even an infant. On each of these points, Ambrose's views were even more radical than those of Augustine. Bodily goods are a distraction to the soul from which the Christian should turn and flee. Death is a relief provided by God from the penal condition into which the human spirit fell by its desire for carnal experience.

The theological outlook of these two bishops made them tolerant of war, particularly when it was waged and won by Christians. This same viewpoint, however, kept them from a glorification of earthly dominion and from a too-easy identification of God's purposes with the fortunes of the Christian Roman Empire.

NOTES

1. F. H. Dudden, *The Life and Times of St. Ambrose* (Oxford: At the Clarendon Press, 1935), 258–69, 344–56, 380–81, 412–34.

2. Symmachus *Memorial* 9; Ambrose *Epistle* 61.62; idem, *On the Death of Theodosius* 7; idem, *Explanation of Psalm* 35 25; Augustine *Against Faustus* 22.76; idem, *On the City of God* 5.26; Orosius *History Against the Pagans* 7.35; Theodoret *Ecclesiastical History* 5.24; Socrates Scholasticus *Ecclesiastical History* 5.24; Sozomen *Ecclesiastical History* 7.24.

3. Ambrose *Epistle* 61.62; idem, *On the Death of Theodosius* 4; Augustine *Against Faustus* 22.76.

4. P. Brown, *Augustine of Hippo* (Berkeley and Los Angeles: University of California Press, 1969), 366–69, 381–89; O. Perler, *Les voyages de saint Augustin* (Paris: Etudes Augustiniennes, 1969), 366–69.

5. *Epistle* 189.

6. *Epistle* 220.

7. *De interpellatione David; On the Death of Theodosius* 39.

8. *Against Faustus* 22.73–78. A brief discussion can be found earlier in *On Free Choice* 1.4.9, 1.15.31–33.

9. *Epistle* 185.

10. The whole of book 19 is relevant; see esp. chaps. 24–28.

Conclusion

In summing up our findings, we are acutely aware of the near impossibility of making a summary or drawing general conclusions that would not, in one important aspect or other, be incomplete, misleading, or even false. This is due both to the matter itself and to the way it is approached by scholars.

Five Phases

The matter itself spans a period of almost four centuries, from the NT to the death of Augustine in 430. Within this period, one can see the church and its members growing and moving through several phases. There was, *first,* the experience of being a new community struggling to grow out of its Jewish background and struggling to become itself in the much broader Greco-Roman context. *Second,* there was the phase—roughly from the Apostolic Fathers to about the time of Origen in the first half of the third century—when Irenaeus, Tertullian, Hippolytus, Cyprian, Clement, and Origen were setting the foundations and framing the structures of Christian theology. During this period, Christians knew themselves, socially and politically, as an insignificant and powerless minority struggling to establish its identity and existence in an inhospitable and sometimes downright hostile world.

This was followed by a *third* phase—unfortunately much neglected by scholars who have reflected on this material—spanning the years from the end of the persecution of Gallienus in the middle of the third century to the beginning of that of Diocletian and Galerius in the beginning of the fourth. This has been described as a period of "peace" so far as the persecution of Christians was concerned. But one must also look beyond that somewhat facile label and see it as a time of "testing." It was a time in which the empire and the still fledgling Christian community apparently began to perceive each other as

87

rivals. The attitude of the empire seemed to become one of tolerance in the expectation or hope that Christianity, left to itself, might just fade away. Increasing numbers of Christians, however, apparently found places in public and even military life. The stage was set for the final great confrontation when Diocletian and Galerius, in their efforts to strengthen the empire internally, tried to impose religious uniformity. By the time Constantine recognized Christianity as a valuable ally in the pursuit of his political ambitions, it was still a minority but, quite obviously, no longer "insignificant" or "powerless."

The *fourth* phase is identified with the names of Constantine and Eusebius. Modern Christian hindsight, especially from the perspective of modern liberal democracies, is embarrassed at the glorified role church leaders like Eusebius attributed to Constantine in the history of salvation. But rather than see this as the church suddenly selling its soul, our study shows that it makes far more sense to see it, polemical and apologetic excesses aside, as a fairly natural and logical development from the kind of experience Christians were having and the kind of reflection they were engaging in throughout the previous century. Origen, as we pointed out, presented what comes closest to a theory of Christian pacifism in the pre-Constantinian church. But, as we also pointed out, the very logic of his argument against Celsus in A.D. 248 drove Christians, in a changed situation, toward the kind of accommodation and cooperation we see beginning to take place under Constantine.

The *fifth* phase is that of "establishment," which we see reflected in the careers and writings of Ambrose and Augustine. This has commonly been described as the church holding the opposite of what it held in the second and third centuries. But when one looks beyond the surface to the changing sociopolitical situations, one can find a fairly consistent and logical thread that does not require us to postulate a massive and not easily explicable transformation.

The five phases we have described might appear somewhat arbitrary and others might easily specify different sequences of phases or periods. The important point is that an awareness of some such set of phases is necessary if one is to begin to do justice to the complexity of the material.

Three Themes

Our study of the early Christian materials has also identified three themes that endured, with minor variations, throughout the five phases we have defined. The first of these is the attitude toward the value of human life. The second involves the appropriate function of war. The third regards the superhuman or divine element in military power and warfare. We shall examine each of these in turn.

First, the destruction of human life and property does not seem to have been a significant consideration for either Christian or pagan. Cicero did not mention it. Augustine explicitly rejected it as a religious consideration. For many Christians, such as Origen, this attitude may have been a consequence of an antimaterial bias or the belief that the present arrangement was a temporary one to be transformed or replaced in the return of Christ. Others considered bodily death a due punishment for a life of sin on the way of entrance to the eternal kingdom of Christ that was to be patiently endured or even desired. Early Christians seem to have considered the achievements of the dominant pagan culture of no lasting value and did not mourn their destruction in warfare.

Second, the purposes and justification of warfare seem to have been much the same for Christians, though they were somewhat different from that of the prevailing pagan culture. Cicero identified two forms of warfare, each of which had a stable peace as its objective. A defensive war might be fought for survival against an enemy bent on destruction. In this instance, almost any means of resistance might be used and a lasting peace might be achieved only through the extermination of the opponent. A second type of war is fought to gain supremacy over a rival state or people. Such a war should be provoked by some legitimating injustice. It must be pursued in a manner that would lay the foundation for lasting peace: prisoners must be protected, promises must be honored, and cruelty must be avoided. The contestants recognize that the outcome is in the hands of the gods and accept defeat with honor intact. The objective of this form of war must be the elimination of a rivalry that threatens the stable peace.

In the first three of the phases we have defined, Christians seem to have regarded the use of military force for the protection of the temporal order as a function proper to the government of the empire. Some served in the army and most accounts of their witness to Christ do not conceal or apologize for their military service to the empire. Others refused military service because they were concerned only with the heavenly kingdom of Christ. Some bishops and theologians urged such a turning from all earthly pursuits while others argued that the proper Christian contribution to the safety of the empire was made through prayer and asceticism rather than military service. In this situation, we do not find discussions of the different forms of warfare and the legitimacy of participation in each. In fact, of course, the empire was largely in a defensive posture through all five phases.

In the fourth phase, Eusebius undertook a theological justification of Constantine's war of conquest. The legitimating objective was a stable peace and the appropriate means to secure it was through establishing a single ruler who would mirror the divine dominion over the universe. Ambrose may have been thinking in the same vein when he condemned rebellion and praised Theodosius for overthrowing usurpers. These were civil wars rather than campaigns to extend dominion over foreign peoples.

Only in Augustine does one find an explicit rejection of the Roman war of conquest. While he recognized that its objective was a stable peace, he charged that it was motivated by a lust for domination. He seems to have approved warfare only for defensive purposes. Like Cicero and Ambrose, he urged that war must be waged in a manner that would enhance a stable peace with the subjugated enemy.

Christians seem to have simply accepted warfare as a fact of life in a sinful world. Some exempted themselves from participation on the grounds that it did not belong to the new existence in Christ. Others, in all five phases or periods, seem to have accepted responsibility for a world that was not yet fully renewed and then took up arms to resist the forces that threatened temporal peace. We have not discovered evidence of a Christian legitimation of a war of foreign domination or conquest.

Third, pagan and Christian seem to have agreed in attributing success in warfare to a divine intervention. As evidenced in the writing of Cicero and in the practices of Roman army religion, this meant that the power of the army depended on a careful and regular cultivation of the gods. Sacrilege or violation of religious protocol would threaten the safety and fighting power of the army. Objections to Christian participation in the army during the second and third phase were largely based upon the supposition that the power operative in the military was demonic. Only in the fourth and fifth phases did Christian theologians assert that military action could be inspired and supported by God. The perceived relation between the divine power and military success should be examined in greater detail in each of these phases.

During the first phase, when Christians were a persecuted minority, we find two responses to the demonic power active in warfare. The love command in the canonical NT calls the Christian to work to free oppressors from the control of the evil forces and win them over to

Christ. The desire for vindication or revenge that is evident in some of the canonical and especially in the apocryphal materials evinces a similar judgment of the true source of persecution. In neither case, however, was the Christian called upon to offer violent resistance. God himself would effect the conversion or overthrow of the persecutor.

In the second phase, when Christians were a tolerated minority, they were urged to refrain from participation in the military because of the connection between military power and the cult of the demons in army religion. Origen asserted that peace is promoted by spiritual attacks on the demons who are the source of hostile military power. Because Christians were not a distinct people, Origen did not expect God to intervene militarily to protect them as he had Israel.

In the second and third phases, we have identified an alternate view. A good number of Christians seem to have served in the Roman army and even participated in its rituals without perceiving a conflict with their commitment to Christ. Some of the officers and judges who were called upon to enforce religious conformity were willing to tolerate a feigned compliance. The accounts of military martyrdoms indicate that many Christians and the officers under whom they served did not perceive a strict connection between the religious cult and the valor or success of the soldiers. Christians stood on their service records and judges attempted to rescue good troops from execution.

In the fourth and fifth phases, Christian theologians continued to find the working of demonic forces in warfare. Christians were becoming a people more easily identifiable with the Roman Empire. Some emperors could be recognized as champions raised up by God for the defense of his church through their military campaigns. In the victories of Constantine, Eusebius saw God intervening to destroy the power of Satan. Ambrose, Augustine, and the later Christian historians make the same judgment of God's operation in Theodosius's victory over Eugenius. In each instance, the OT notion of a chosen people served as the interpretative category.

In the fifth phase, Ambrose and Augustine perceived the danger of the demonic forces working within the Christian rulers. Ambrose called Theodosius to repent a massacre at Thessalonica he had ordered in anger and Augustine decried the effects of lust, greed, and ambition in Boniface. Augustine asserted that God controls all events in the temporal sphere and bestows material goods according to his own design. God promotes the salvation of his people not only by victory but even by defeat and death. This analysis recognized a divine role in warfare but refused to place God at the service of his people's ambition or even their desire for secure enjoyment of earthly goods.

Christian theologians, like their pagan counterparts, were convinced that military victory involved more than human power.

In the first three phases, however, the Christians seem not to have expected that God would intervene through military means to achieve his purposes; they were convinced that the true battle was fought only on the spiritual plane. The story of the Thundering Legion constitutes a singular exception. In a similar way, many Christian soldiers did not perceive any connection between their faith in Christ and their military activity. Only in the fourth and fifth phases did Christian theologians assert that God intervenes against the demonic power by military means.

In these three areas we find both continuity and difference between the various phases of Christian thought and practice. The analysis indicates, however, that in each phase the Christian doctrine was shaped by the interaction of faith in Christ and a particular sociopolitical setting. No Christian attitudes toward the military, even those in the canonical NT, were independent of their cultural context.

Our own age may seem discontinuous with all of these early Christian attitudes. We have a different valuation of human life on earth and of the cultural achievements which are destroyed by war. We are threatened with the destruction of the human species and of the earth as a host for living beings. War no longer appears an appropriate instrument for achieving peace and protecting the enjoyment of earthly goods. Although we may not regard them as demonic agents, we are increasingly convinced of the role of social evils, of passions or vices shared by whole peoples, as the sources of war and destroyers of peace. The origin of war in human sin is evident but the divine use of military power to limit and overcome that evil is increasingly questioned. Some Christians have recourse to the prayer and asceticism Origen recommended while others labor to implement the love command through international agreements and even the deterrent of threatened mutual assured destruction.

Using the Sources

When we turn to sources of Christian truth for guidance, to the scriptures and their interpretations in the early church, we are struck not only by the complexity of the matter itself and of the contexts in which it is found, but also by the variety of presuppositions and methods with which it is retrieved and presented. Most Christians accept the Bible, especially the NT, and to a lesser but nonetheless real extent, the teaching and practice of the early church as normative for Christian life. But there is a tremendous variety in how Christians understand their function. One can mean literally normative, or generally normative, or inceptively normative, or negatively normative, etc. The vast pluralism of positions from which different Christians approach the Bible, from an overly simplified literal biblicism to an overly critical rationalist reductionism, come into play here. The shifting spectrum from biblicism to reductionism is by no means the only variant at work, however. For example, one finds at the biblicist end of the spectrum not only radical pacifists but also just-war theorists and even holy-war proponents. They have in common the false methodological assumption that the teaching and the practice of the Bible and early church, without analysis of sociological and historical context, and without the application of a balanced hermeneutic is literally normative for contemporary teaching and practice. They assume that whatever they perceive the Bible and early church to have been, that is what modern Christians must also be. But after this common assumption, tremendous variety comes from their personal and community faith positions that provide them with antennae sensitive only to a certain range of data. The nonsupporting data are unrecognized, ignored, or even misinterpreted in the cause of supporting the "true" Christian position. This has the general, sad effect of discrediting much Christian witness in the eyes of those who have no axes, or simply different axes, to grind.

It is one of the characteristics of this book that its different authors came to it with, so to speak, different axes to grind. Aware of that, and taking advantage of that diversity, we have tried to make a more adequate, more faithful, more true presentation of the teaching, witness, and experience of the early Christians on the issue of war and military service. If history, philosophy, and theology teach us anything, then it is that no lasting peace can be built on anything less than truth. We hope to have freed the cause of peace and the truth that grounds it from some of the burden of mistaken assumptions and misread history that has tended to weigh it down in the past.

Bibliography

A select list of the works which the authors found the most helpful in preparing this volume.

Alföldi, Andras. *The Conversion of Constantine and Pagan Rome,* trans. H. Mattingly. Oxford: Clarendon Press, 1948.

Balthasar, Hans Urs von. *Origen. Spirit and Fire: A Thematic Anthology of His Writings,* trans. R. Daly. Washington: Catholic University of America Press, 1984.

Brown, Peter. *Religion and Society in the Age of Saint Augustine.* New York: Harper & Row, 1972. See especially the articles on religious coercion, 260-78, 301-31.

Bainton, Roland H. *Christian Attitudes Toward War and Peace.* Nashville: Abingdon Press, 1960.

Berchem, Andreas. *Le martyre de la Légion Thébaine.* Schweizerische Beiträge zur Altertumswissenschaft 8. Basel, 1968.

Bigelmair, Andreas. *Die Beteiligung der Christen am öffentlichen Leben in vorconstantinischer Zeit.* Veröffentlichungen aus dem Kirchenhistorischen Seminar München 8. Reihe 1. no. 8. Munich: J. J. Lentner, 1902.

Brand, Clarence R. *Roman Military Law.* Austin: University of Texas Press, 1968.

Cadoux, Cecil J. *The Early Christian Attitude to War.* London, 1919; New York: Seabury Press, 1982.

Campenhausen, Hans von. "Christians and Military Service in the Early Church" in *Tradition and Life in the Church,* trans. A. V. Littledale. Philadelphia: Fortress Press, 1968.

Caspary, Gerard E. *Politics and Exegesis: Origen and the Two Swords.* Berkeley and London: University of California Press, 1979.

Crouzel, Henri. "Origen and Origenism." *New Catholic Encyclopedia* 10, 767–74.

Daly, Robert, et al. *Christian Biblical Ethics: From Biblical Revelation to Contemporary Christian Praxis: Method and Content.* New York and Ramsey, N.J.: Paulist Press, 1984.

Davies, R. W. "Police Work in Roman Times." *History Today* 18 (1968): 700–707.

Delehaye, Hippolyte. *Les legendes grecques des saints militaires.* Paris, 1909; New York: Arno, 1975.

Diesner, Hans-Joachim. *Kirche und Staat im spätrömischen Reich.* Berlin: Evangelische Verlagsanstalt, 1963. Pp. 100–26 deal with the career of Count Boniface.

Domaszewski, Alfred von. "Die Religion des römischen Heeres." *Westdeutsche Zeitschrift für Geschichte und Kunst* 14, 1 (1895): 1–121.

Fink, Robert O. *Roman Military Records on Papyrus.* Philological Monographs of the American Philological Association 26. Cleveland: Case Western Reserve, 1971.

Fontaine, Jacques, ed. *Q. Septimi Florentis Tertulliani de Corona.* Paris: Presses universitaires de France, 1966.

Grant, Robert M. "War—Just, Holy, Unjust—in Hellenistic and Early Christian Thought." *Augustinianum* 20 (1980): 173–89.

Harnack, Adolf von. *Militia Christi,* trans. D. M. Gracie. Philadelphia: Fortress Press, 1981.

Helgeland, John. "Roman Army Religion." *Aufstieg und Niedergang der römischen Welt (ANRW)* II.16.1 (1978). Berlin and New York: Walter de Gruyter.

Helgeland, John. "Christians in the Roman Army, A.D. 173–337." *ANRW* II.23.1 (1979).

Hoey, Allan S. "Official Policy Towards Oriental Cults in the Roman Army." *Transactions and Proceedings of the American Philological Association* 70 (1939): 456–81.

Hornus, Jean Michel. *It Is Not Lawful for Me to Fight: Early Christian Attitudes Toward War, Violence, and the State.* Scottdale, Pa.: Herald Press, 1980.

Jones, Arnold H. M. *The Later Roman Empire, 284–602: A Social, Economic, and Administrative Survey.* 2 vols. Norman, Okla.: University of Oklahoma Press, 1964.

Klein, Richard. "Tertullian und das römische Reich." *Bibliothek der klassischen Altertumswissenschaften.* n.F., 2. Reihe, Bd. 22. Heidelberg: C. Winter, 1968.

Leclercq, Henry. "Militarisme." *Dictionnaire d'archéologie chrétienne et de liturgie,* ed. Cabrol and Leclercq, 2:2692–2703. Paris: Letourzey et Ané, 1923.

MacMullen, Ramsay. *Constantine.* New York: Dial, 1969.

MacMullen, Ramsay. *Soldier and Civilian in the Later Roman Empire.* Cambridge: Harvard University Press, 1967.

Markus, Robert A. *Saeculum: History and Society in the Theology of St. Augustine.* Cambridge: Cambridge University Press, 1970.

Moffat, J. "War." *Dictionary of the Apostolic Church,* ed. J. Hastings, 2:646–73. New York: Charles Scribner's Sons, 1918.

Musurillo, Herbert. *The Acts of the Christian Martyrs.* New York: Oxford University Press, 1972.

Nock, Arthur D. "The Roman Army and the Religious Year." *Harvard Theological Review* 45 (1952): 187–252.

Parker, Henry M. D. *The Roman Legions.* Oxford, 1928; Cambridge: Heffer, 1958.

Perkins, Pheme. *Love Commandments in the New Testament.* New York and Ramsey, N.J.: Paulist Press, 1982.

Peterson, E. "Blitz und Regenwunder an der Marcus-Säule." *Rheinisches Museum für Philologie* 50 (1895): 453–74.

Regout, Robert. *La doctrine de la guerre juste de saint Augustin à nos jours, d'après les théologiens et les canonistes catholiques.* Paris: Editions Pedone, 1934; Aalen: Scientia, 1974.

Ryan, Edward A. "The Rejection of Military Service by the Early Christians." *Theological Studies* 13 (1952): 1–32.

Schottroff, Luise. "Non-Violence and the Love of One's Enemies" in *Essays on the Love Commandment,* trans. R. H. Fuller and I. Fuller. Philadelphia: Fortress Press, 1978.

Stevenson, James. *A New Eusebius: Documents Illustrative of the Church to A.D. 337.* London: SPCK, 1968.

Swift, Louis J. *The Early Fathers on War and Military Service.* Message of the Fathers of the Church 19. Wilmington, Del.: Michael Glazier, 1983.

Watson, George R. *The Roman Soldier.* Ithaca, N.Y.: Cornell University Press, 1969.

Webster, Graham G. *The Roman Imperial Army of the First and Second Centuries A.D.* London: A. & C. Black, 1969.

Index